NASCAR Wives:
THE WOMEN BEHIND THE SUNDAY DRIVERS

BY LIZ ALLISON

This book is dedicated to the ladies presented in these pages and to those who many years ago paved the way for the participation of females in the National Association for Stock Car Auto Racing. All of these women are truly the backbone of the sport. Their love for their families and their own dedication to NASCAR competition are invaluable to the men who sacrifice so much to give us the most exciting sport in the world.

(Editor's Note: This book profiles women married to men who race, or have raced, in NASCAR's primary division, which was founded as the "Strictly Stock" circuit in 1949. It was quickly renamed the "Grand National Series" and officially became the "NASCAR Winston Cup Series" in the mid-1980s. For the sake of clarity, the most recent designation is used throughout herein.)

ACKNOWLEDGEMENTS

UMI Publications is both pleased and proud to present *NASCAR Wives: The Women Behind The Sunday Drivers*. UMI and Liz Allison, the author of this book owe its inception, development and creation to so many people, all who should be mentioned here.

To all those whose stories appear here, the author admires them more than they can imagine. Their strengths are many and weaknesses are few. While they represent different eras in the history of the sport, all of them deserve medals.

Betty Jane France, Lesa France Kennedy and Patti Wheeler all taught the writer how to be a lady in a man's world. Each is a class act and dear friend. A very special mention goes to Jennifer White of NASCAR, who encouraged and inspired the author.

We would be remiss without acknowledging the hard work of NASCAR's Bill, Jim, and Brian France, Mike Helton, Paul Brooks, George Pyne, Jim Hunter, Steve Boguski and Paul Schaefer.

Thanks, also, to David Green, Jim Huber, Neil Sims, Ben White, Deb Williams and Larry Woody — the best teachers in the world — each an inspiration from whom the writer learned so much. And the knowledge imparted by Jim Freeman of the International Motorsports Hall of Fame is immeasurable.

The writer sends a "big hug" to her friends at TNT, NASCAR.com and NBC for lassoing her back into the sport she loves. Without Alden Webb and Mike Vaden, she'd be lost. The same applies to her Tuesday-morning prayer group. Everyone — Diane, Donna, Georgia, Kathy, Kelly, Linda, Mary, Pammy and Patti — have taught her the meaning of friendship.

The author recognizes Ryan as her love and constant cheerleader. He must be tired by now! Her mother and father get the "red-line" award for always accepting her phone calls and listening to her stories when they didn't have time. Krista and Robbie sacrificed so much for their mommy to do yet "another book." The author thanks God for blessing her with the two most precious human beings ever. How did she get so lucky?

The writer, most importantly, offers eternal thanks to her Heavenly Father for keeping her in the passenger seat when she was trying to be the driver. Every prayer has been answered and she is so blessed!

UMI Staff
President and Publisher, *Ivan Mothershead;* Vice President and Associate Publisher, *Charlie Keiger;* Associate Publisher, *Rick Peters;* Controller, *Lewis Patton;* Chief Operating Officer & Vice President and National Advertising Manager, *Mark Cantey;* Advertising Executive, *Paul Kaperonis;* Managing Editor, *Ward Woodbury;* Associate Editor, *Gary McCredie;* Senior Editor, *Bob Kelly;* Art Director, *Brett Shippy;* Senior Designer, *Paul Bond;* Manager of Information Systems, *Chris Devera;* Administrative Staff: *Mary Flowe, Heather Guy, Melody Plyler, Amy Tosco and Renee Wedvick.* Shipping & Receiving, *Glen Guy.*

Preproduction work provided by ISCOA (International Scanning Corporation of America)

NASCAR Wives: The Women Behind The Sunday Drivers is Officially Licensed by NASCAR.

ISBN: 0-943860-21-0

FOREWORD
BY BETTY JANE FRANCE

*A*lthough I lived in the heart of racing country *as a young teenager, I had little interest in the activities at the local track in my hometown of Winston-Salem, N.C. I agreed to enter the Miss Bowman Gray Stadium pageant with no great expectations, thinking it would be at least fun. I truly had no idea I was about to become intimately involved in a sport that would eventually gain the respect and attention of the entire world.*

Much to my surprise, I won the contest; more importantly, through that experience I met two couples who were to have a strong and enduring influence on me. Bill France Sr. and his wife, Anne, and their friends, Alvin and Eloise Hawkins, had together brought NASCAR to Winston-Salem. Through them, I soon acquired a deep appreciation for the many complicated aspects of putting on a racing event. Meeting a handsome, charming official named Bill France Jr. no doubt also contributed to my fascination with NASCAR.

I quickly learned that Mrs. France and Mrs. Hawkins were intelligent, practical women, respected by and depended upon by their husbands. They were strong, effective business partners as well as loving wives and mothers. When I married Bill and moved to Daytona, Anne France became my mother-in-law, teacher and mentor. She helped me find my own place and guided me through the challenges of working and raising a family in a high profile, fast-paced ever-evolving sport.

As I recollect my personal journey, I think about all the courageous racing wives I've known and watched through the years. Being married to a driver presents a unique set of thrills and heartaches. Some women would choose such a life, while others would endure it for the sake of a husband's dream. Certainly, each woman in this book has contributed in her own way to the perception of NASCAR as a sport where spouses and families are honored.

I appreciate and admire them all.

Betty Jane France
Assistant Secretary, NASCAR

NASCAR Wives:
The Women Behind The Sunday Drivers

by Liz Allison

Table of Contents

Intro by Liz Allison	6		Kim Labonte	92
Judy Allison	14		Wanda Lund	98
Nancy Andretti	20		Paula Marlin	104
Diane Bodine	26		Arlene Martin	110
Lynn Bodine	32		Andrea Nemechek	116
Susan Bonnett	38		Lynda Petty	122
Kim Burton	44		Pattie Petty	128
Tabitha Burton	50		Doris Roberts	134
Catherine Craven	56		Linda Rudd	140
Cindy Elliott	62		Ann Schrader	146
Frances Flock	68		Angela Skinner	152
DeLana Harvick	74		Pat Spencer	158
Jina Jones	80		Bunny Turner	164
Donna Labonte	86		Buffy Waltrip	170

INTRODUCTION
BY LIZ ALLISON

I, like all the women in this book spent a part of my life as a race car driver's wife. It seems like just yesterday that I was chasing my own children around the speedway infield and juggling my time between being a wife and mom. Crazy as it was, I will cherish those times as some of the most special in my life.

It all started for me when I was 22 years old. I was born in Augusta, Ga., but living in Charleston, S.C., going to school and working. I had a dear friend, who was dating a guy whose family owned a short track in Summerville, northwest of Charleston. This particular night in August 1988 was different from other nights because the Winston Cup boys were coming to Summerville Speedway to run a celebrity race, which was part of an annual program called the "Tiny Lund Memorial." I didn't know it at the time but Tiny was a NASCAR driver who had been killed years before in Talladega, Ala. His widow, Wanda, would later become a very special friend to me.

Rusty Wallace, Rodney Combs, Phil Parsons and Davey Allison were there to run in a "shoot out" and sign autographs. Then it was back to nearby Darlington Raceway where they would be racing on Sunday in the Southern 500.

I was sitting on the back of a friend's truck when Davey jumped up on its bed and grabbed my hand to see if I was married. Now, I have to tell you I was not sure what had just happened to me. First of all, here was a stranger wearing corduroys and a jacket in the steaming Low Country heat and humidity while the rest of us were dying; secondly, I was not sure about his boldness. It seemed that about the time I opened my mouth to say something he grabbed my hand and pulled me over to the car he was about to drive in the race. He took off his hat, handed it to me and asked me to hold it for him while he raced. To this day I don't remember saying either yes or no. Before I knew it he was racing and I was holding that hat like it was a fine piece of china.

Afterward, he pulled right up to where I was standing and asked me for my phone number. Not knowing if he really would call or not — and not quite sure how my roommate would respond to a stranger calling — I gave him my work number. He was whisked away by security, but before he left he leaned down and kissed me on the cheek and told me to watch him on TV Sunday.

I felt like a whirlwind just went by me. I think I sat there for a minute to catch my breath, but before too long my friends starting saying, "Do you know who that was? Did you see the way he looked at you?" I myself was uncertain of our meeting and went on my way, not sure if I would ever see or hear from him again. I decided that I probably wouldn't.

I was at work a few days later when I heard the secretary say: "Hey Liz you have a call on line one. It's somebody with an accent by the name of Davey." I could not believe my ears. He had called just like he said he would, only he was a little confused as to why he had a work number. I didn't bother to explain why. It wasn't long before I had some explaining to do to my roommate, though, as Davey started calling me at my apartment once or twice a week and I suddenly quit the "singles" dating scene. My friends wanted to know who or what had changed my life because something was quite different about me. I knew it, too; I just wasn't ready to admit to it.

Davey and I met in August and it was November

(Opposite page) Liz Allison was married to a prominent NASCAR Winston Cup Series driver, and her children — Krista Marie and Robert Grey — were born into the sport. She knows what it's like to raise a family while being away from home much of the year and has experienced the triumphs and tragedies that a life in motorsports can bring. Today, remarried, she makes her home in Nashville, Tenn.

Under the attentive eyes of his mom, Robert gets an idea of what his dad does for a living.

before I would see him again. He had been traveling the racing circuit and spending as much time as possible with his dad, Bobby Allison, who was still recovering from a very serious racing accident in June of that year.

We made plans for me to come to the Atlanta race at the end of the 1988 season. Even though I'd talked to Davey almost every day before I got to Atlanta, I was quite nervous about seeing him again. My fears were put to rest when we met. It was as if we had never been apart. I guess you can say it was love at first sight because what we felt that night in Summerville made enough of an impression to keep us together, even though we were miles apart for three months.

Things went pretty quick from that point on. The twice-a-week calls turned into daily conversations, and our visits increased to every other week. I'd see him when I could or he'd skip into Charleston for a night when his scheduled allowed. One night, I was in the tub soaking after a long day at work. Charlotte, my roommate, knocked on the door to tell me Davey was on the telephone. She said it sounded like he was in an airplane or something because it was so loud. I got to the phone with dripping hair and a towel wrapped around me. He said, "You better come get me. I'm landing at the Mt. Pleasant airport in 15 minutes." I thought he was pulling my leg and continued to dry off. He became more insistent: "Are you going to come get me, or am I going to have to take a cab?" I realized he was as crazy as I thought but joyfully went to retrieve him. After getting lost three times on back roads I finally found the airport — and it was closed! I looked everywhere for Davey and finally spotted him asleep on the bench outside of the gates. He was not amused with my tardiness. It had been over an hour since I left home. "Nice of you to hurry," he said.

Davey was into his third year in Winston Cup racing and was quite successful and very busy. I worked during the week and left on Friday after work to be with him wherever the race might be. There were many times that I would drive all night to get there. Sometimes, I'd show up at the track Saturday morning and grab a few hours of sleep in the car before racing would start. My grandmother used to say, "You can't drive 10 minutes to see your family, but you will drive 500 miles to see Davey." How true that was. I had to be with him. My family knew how much I loved him and how miserable I was when I was not with him. So they tried their best to understand my desire to race across the country just to follow Davey's career.

Davey and I had discussed perhaps getting married one day, and he even offered somewhat of an informal proposal in Richmond, Va., in March 1989. It would, however, be in Charlotte one evening after dinner that the "real thing" would come.

I went to the Queen City that spring of to see Davey, who was living in Alabama but was there on business. After we left the restaurant he drove me back to my hotel and just blurted out, "I love you. Will you marry me?" I was so excited, I jumped up and down and screamed in his ear until he finally said, "Does this mean yes?"

Davey was a very impulsive person, as I would find out more times than not over the course of our life together. We were engaged but had not made definite wedding plans yet when Davey decided he did not want to wait any longer. I was in Alabama with him one day for a brief visit when he grabbed his cousin, Tommy, and myself and said, "Come on. We are going to get married right now." I was shocked beyond belief but there was no argument from me. It would just be to my family I would have to do some explaining. Davey and I were married on Aug. 30, 1989 in the courthouse in Bessemer, Ala., with Tommy alongside of us.

Davey and I rented an apartment in Hueytown, Ala., near his Busch Series race shop. Davey's entire family was there — I'd guess you say it was home base for the "Alabama Gang" — and he was adamant about raising our children where he grew up. That was an important issue, as Davey and I were expecting our first child. We were so excited about just the thought of being parents and attended childbirth classes together. I would, however, get upset when he was supposed to be paying attention but instead would be signing autographs — although it was humorous!

Liz, Krista and Robert enjoyed several of Davey's victories, including the International Race of Champions (IROC), a special series pitting leading drivers from various forms of racing against each other in similarly-prepared cars of the same make. Davey was awarded the 1993 title posthumously.

The Allisons enjoyed Davey's success in Winston Cup racing. He rose to the top quickly and was one of the sport's most well liked personalities.

Davey and I chose not to know the sex of our child before its birth. He'd always say, "If God meant for us to know what we were having then your belly would have a window." There was no way to argue that point.

Krista Marie Allison was born on Dec. 24 just a few hours before Christmas Day. After the nursed cleaned her up, she was brought to us in a Christmas stocking that I still have today. Davey had never shined like he did when Krista, and later, Robbie, were born.

Davey and I decided we needed a bigger place but had only been talking about it. Then my spontaneous husband came home one evening and announced (very happily I might add) that he had bought something for me that day. I was eager to receive my gift but was not expecting what I was about to hear. Davey, in his always excited way, said, "I bought you a

house." I have to admit I was under the assumption that when a couple buys a house, they pick it out together. Davey said, "Do you want to go see it?" Luckily for him, I loved the house. Actually, it was perfect for our little family. There was just one problem: Our family was about to get larger, so we'd need a bigger place pretty quickly.

We lived in that house for a short time and then started building a home. The site consisted of several acres, wasn't far from where we lived and afforded us the opportunity to build the home of our dreams. The construction process went on much longer than we expected, and our second child, Robert Grey "Robbie" Allison, was born July 30, 1991. We finally moved into our home in January 1993.

I was still trying to travel the circuit with Davey as much as I could but our small children certainly threw us a curveball. We had our own airplane by this time, but there was still the problem of situating ourselves at the track to watch the race. Robbie and Krista were only 18 months apart so finding a place for yourself and two babies was difficult. I would pal up with some of my girlfriends who had small children as well. I remember at North Wilkesboro (N.C.) Speedway one time Ann Schrader, Paula Marlin and myself put the kids in a playpen in the garage area near turn one, put earplugs in their ears and let them play to their little hearts' content. My other dear friends were Linda McReynolds and Diane Bodine. Larry McReynolds was Brett Bodine's crew chief on the Kenny Bernstein/Quaker State team when we all became friends. Davey used to kid me about what team I was cheering for.

Sometimes Liz, who was responsible for two small children, had to use a little "technology" to keep up with her husband's activities.

Racing was good to us, but it would be 1992 that would change our lives. We began the year by renewing our wedding vows, finally getting that church wedding my family always wanted. But, it was all downhill from there. Davey was winning but was in several really bad racing accidents. He spent that season either in victory lane or the infield care center. It was a terrible year. Then in August 1992 Davey's younger brother, Clifford, crashed during a Busch Series practice session at Michigan International Speedway and died shortly afterwards. This was the worst thing to ever happen to the entire Allison family. Davey was devastated by Clifford's death and never got over the loss.

It was after Clifford's passing that Davey took up another hobby — piloting helicopters. He eventually purchased a copter for quick trips to and from the airport. I never liked the idea and it became a constant point of contention between us. I felt helicopters weren't safe and subsequently wouldn't let Davey fly with our children.

Davey could never get enough racing. On his day off, he decided to watch David Bonnett, the son of Neil and Susan Bonnett, test a car at Talladega. He got into his helicopter with Red Farmer, a race driver and old Allison family friend, for the 15-minute flight to the track. Davey was attempting to land in the speedway's infield when he lost control of the machine. He and Red slammed the ground with such force that the bystanders felt the ground shake. Red was pulled from the wreckage with non-life threatening injuries, but Davey was not as lucky. He was air-lifted to Carraway Medical

Liz credits her friends for guiding her through difficult times, staying involved in life and reestablishing a presence in racing. (Above) From left: Susan Bonnett; Susan's friend, Edith Bracknell; Liz' mom, Betty Mayson, Liz and Diane Bodine. (Below): Liz (left) with Judy Allison and Bunny Turner Hall.

Center in Birmingham. I realized early on that he wouldn't survive. My heart broke for Robbie, Krista, myself and everyone else who knew Davey. Our two precious children, who adored their Daddy more than anything, would never be held by him again. After a grueling 16 hours Davey was pronounced dead.

I went into a whirlwind as I struggled to survive those first few years. I moved my children to Tennessee to be closer to family and friends. I pulled away from racing, as it was much too painful for me to experience without Davey. My dear racing friends never gave up on me, even though life had changed so much for the kids and me. I was only 28 and had two young children. I had to make some plans for survival. I remember feeling like my life had been shredded into a million pieces. I was so completely lost.

The Good Lord pulled me through the painful loss of my husband and kept me on course through the rough waters of grief and single parenthood. But we all made it. I threw myself into raising my children and writing, which is what led me to my newly discovered passion and a career. In January 2000, I was contacted by Jim Huber of TNT Sports. He asked if I would be interested in being a reporter for Winston Cup and Busch Series races. I accepted, and here I am today, once again traveling the circuit with my dear friends. My grandmother once told me, "If you hang around long enough, life will make a full circle," and it certainly did just that.

I'm now remarried to a wonderful man, Ryan Hackett, who loves my children as his own. Robbie is 10 years old, doing a little racing himself and is a spitting image of Davey. Krista is 12. She is a "Little Liz," as everyone calls her, and is the best cheerleader you have ever seen. We live in Nashville where we try to stay focused on what really matters in life — faith, family, friends and a whole lot of love.

I will never forget my life as Davey Allison's wife. That dreadful day in July 1993 certainly changed my life forever, but I feel completely blessed to have been such a big part of his time here on earth. He was a remarkable person. If you were ever lucky enough to have met him, you just somehow knew you were better off for it. There is still a part of Davey with me everyday.

It is with respect to my years as a driver's wife that I've written this book. I hope you enjoy it.

(Left) Liz and husband Ryan Hackett live in Nashville.

(Above) Here, interviewing driver Andy Belmont, Liz is now involved in a new career — television broadcasting.

JUDY ALLISON

It was a warm Southern California day when Judy Allison, at the age of 33 and accompanied by her husband, Bobby, went back to San Jose to see the house in which she was born. As she looked around and reminisced she realized life had certainly followed some wonderful paths since her birth in November 1944. Her life had also taken many torturous turns that she would have never imagined possible in those early innocent years of her childhood.

Judy Bjorkman and her family moved from California to Fort Lauderdale, Fla., when she was 4 years old. She, her mom and three sisters made a home in the Sunshine State as her father traveled quite frequently for his employer, DuPont.

Childhood was nothing out the ordinary for Judy. She was busy going to school and doing odd jobs here and there for money. But how did she meet her future husband? It seems there are two entirely different stories. Bobby is convinced that while Judy, then 13, was busy sweeping the floor in the race shop of Ralph Stark, he, himself just 20 at the time, came in to see Stark and met her — although the encounter was brief. Bobby was racing for Stark, who was married to Judy's sister, Carolyn.

Judy, however, has no recollection of the incident.

"I was close to 16 years old when I headed to the Medley Speedway in West Hollywood, Fla.," she said. "My brother-in-law had some guys racing the 1X cars and I was sitting in the grandstands when this guy by the name of Bob Jannelle walked up with two girls on his arms. One of the girls was Bobby's date, and they sat down right in front of me."

Bobby crashed during the race and his car caught fire. When he wrecked, Judy jumped up and called out his name. After the race was over Jannelle ran up to Bobby to tell him what Judy had done and then pointed her out to him. After the brief visual encounter between the two, everyone headed to a local hangout to eat. Judy was there with her friends and Bobby came in with a date. He sat at a table directly across from her where he made sure he was facing her, conveniently so she could see him and his date.

Just a few nights later Judy was at her sister's house when there was a knock at the door. There stood Bobby, as Judy remembers "all slicked up," which was out of the ordinary for him. He was there to supposedly talk to Ralph Stark about a car part, when she knew full well he knew where the shop was. He asked Judy to ride with him to Ralph's shop. Judy, who was dating someone at the time, was a little taken back by his forwardness. Even so, she did think he was

---

(Left) A young couple just starting out, Judy and Bobby were married in 1960 and began life in suburban Florida. (Opposite page) Bobby and Judy today. The couple endured terrible tragedy that drove them apart but ultimately set their problems aside and reunited.

kind of cute and decided there was no harm in a short ride.

When they got to the shop it was closed. There was no one to be found anywhere so the two sat and chatted for a while. "All he did was talk about other girls. My reaction was that he was conceited, and I remember telling myself that I didn't ever want to see him again," she said.

A few weeks passed before the two ran across each other again, this time at West Palm Beach Speedway. As fate would have it, Bobby had engine problems and fell out of his race early. He made his way to the grandstands to sit with Judy for the rest of the show and then offered to give her a ride home. Judy didn't know how to respond since she was dating someone else at the time. She asked her sister, Arleen, and Arleen's husband, Hank, what to do. They told her to go with Bobby and so she did. After stopping to eat, they drove to her home, parked out front and talked until 5:30 a.m. As Judy remembers it, her mother was not amused — and rightly so — because they were scheduled to leave the house and move to Orlando — in 30 minutes! "She was so mad at me and I could not blame her, but I did not want to stop talking to him," Judy said.

Bobby promised to come see her in Orlando but Judy could not help but wonder if she would ever see him again. She would not have to wait long to find out. A week later after Bobby finished racing he drove to Orlando and parked in Judy's sister's driveway, waiting for somebody to wake up. "I had curlers in my hair and my sister hollered out to me to get out of bed

Years of struggle and hard work finally paid dividends for the Allisons in 1983 when Bobby won the NASCAR Winston Cup championship. They were the center of attention at the awards banquet in New York that December.

because Bobby was in the drive," Judy said. "I could not believe it." Bobby started driving from South Florida to Orlando (over 200 miles one way) to see Judy every other week as they continued to date for over a year. Then Judy moved back to West Hollywood.

Judy attended a school for beauticians while Bobby continued to race. He came to her graduation ceremony and they went to her sister Carolyn's house after the ceremony. That's where he pulled a little box with a ring in it from his pocket and proposed to her. "I had no idea and I was so excited. It was a pretty good size ring for that time too. I was shocked," said Judy of that special moment.

Bobby and Judy were married in 1960. Bobby paid for the entire wedding, and Judy's mom made her dress. They rented a little house in Oakland Park, a town just north of Fort Lauderdale, and Judy quit working so she could travel to the races with her new husband. The marriage ceremony was still fresh in their minds when Judy suffered a miscarriage, which was devastating because they very much wanted to start a family. Just a few months later Judy became pregnant with what would be her first child. David Carl Allison was born in Hollywood, Fla., February 25, 1961.

Bobby began traveling to Alabama where the racing was more competitive and the money was better. Judy drove with her sister-in-law, Pat Allison, to Birmingham when Davey was just five months old to see her husband race for the first time as a new mom. It was apparent to her that racing with a baby in tow made things a bit more complicated.

Bobby and Judy bought a house in West Hollywood and stayed there as they again expanded their family with the birth of their first daughter, Bonnie, in December 1962. With Bobby racing more often in Alabama, Bobby and Judy decided to relocate to the Birmingham area. They moved into their first house in suburban Hueytown when Bonnie was just five months old. Bobby was racing as many as four nights a week, and Judy went with him as much as she could until Davey started school. During this time, Bobby and Judy welcomed two more children, Clifford in October 1964 and then Carrie in May 1967.

The couple's early years in racing are still some of which Judy cherishes the most. Her best

(Left) Bobby was riding high after winning the fall 1983 400-lap race in Richmond, Va. He also won there that February.

(Below) Bobby drove for team owner Bud Moore (left) from 1978-80 and won 10 NASCAR Winston Cup races. Among them was the 1980 Firecracker 400 at Daytona Beach, Fla., where Judy (third from right) joined him in victory lane.

friends in the sport were Bettie Panch, the wife of race driver Marvin Panch and Martha Jarrett the spouse of two-time NASCAR Winston Cup champion Ned Jarrett. In later years she befriended Stevie Waltrip and Colleen Baker. "All of us girls stuck together back then because we did not have anyone else. We all understood each other so well," said Judy.

Eventually, NASCAR allowed the women to keep track of the laps their husbands ran in races, which is exactly what most of them did. "We started scoring for our husbands so we

Generations. The leader of the "Alabama Gang" is flanked by brother Donnie (left) and friend and protégé Neil Bonnett, while joining them are second-generation "gang" members Hut Stricklin (left), Davey Allison (center) and Mickey Gibbs.

could be involved in their racing. It did keep us out of the infield and it made us feel like we were helping with our husbands' careers," said Judy.

Bobby ran his first four NASCAR Winston Cup races in 1961 but wouldn't compete again in NASCAR's top series until 1965. The next year, though, he went full time on the circuit, won three times and "officially" kicked off one of the most successful careers in the sport. This, however, began to change things for Judy. Their children were getting older and it became more difficult for her to travel with Bobby as she did when they were younger. So Judy spent more time at home and only went racing when she could.

Davey had always been interested in his dad's profession and had been working towards his goal of one day racing against him. He continued on his climb through the lower divisions, which made it even more difficult for Judy to spread her time between her son's quickly expanding involvement in NASCAR and her husband's racing. Before she knew it, it was 1987. Davey had a full-time NASCAR Winston Cup ride and was living out his dreams. "Those were some special times for all of us but especially for Davey and Bobby. They loved racing each other," Judy recalled. "Bobby was so proud of Davey and Davey loved his dad. He was his hero." Judy never worried about Bobby's or Davey's safety. "They both had many wrecks and they were always OK. Even though you know you probably should worry about them on the track, I really didn't that much. I felt like they were smart drivers and would be all right."

It was Fathers Day, June 19, 1988, at Pocono (Pa.) Raceway. The Miller High Life 500 had just begun when Bobby's Buick suddenly slowed, made contact with the wall and was T-boned by another car before the first lap had been completed. He was removed from the wreckage and flown to Lehigh Valley Medical Center in nearby Allentown, where he was listed in critical condition. Judy was told that he would probably not survive, and if he did he would never be like she knew him before the accident. "We did not know what to do," Judy said. "Bobby had always taken care of all of us; now we needed to take care of him but we didn't know how. That was a terrible day. I had never felt so helpless."

Bobby spent three weeks in intensive care and then constant care for another three weeks. He was then flown to Lakeshore Rehabilitation Hospital in Birmingham where he spent yet

another six weeks. His long and successful racing career had come to an end. Years of physical therapy and support from Judy, her kids and the extended Allison family got him back on his feet again where he did return to racing for several years as a car owner.

As Bobby continued his long recovery, Davey and Clifford were both racing. Davey was on the NASCAR Winston Cup circuit and Clifford was running ARCA and NASCAR Busch Series races. Judy found herself completely overwhelmed with Bobby's recovery and her sons' racing. "I had to try to be everything to everybody and I just could not do it. I was very tired and worn down during that time in my life," she admitted.

Davey survived a wicked, bone-breaking crash at Pocono in July 1992, exactly four years and a month after his dad's accident there in 1988. He required relief drivers for the next few races but was still well on his way toward a possible first NASCAR Winston Cup Series championship. Clifford was pursuing his own career and had landed a deal to run a NASCAR Busch Series race at Michigan International Speedway that August. It was half of a scheduled Busch-NASCAR Winston Cup Series weekend at the two-mile oval. During a practice session two days before the Aug. 15 event, Clifford lost control of his car and slammed into the wall. He was killed instantly. Clifford left behind a wife and three children not to mention a mother, father and three siblings, who were devastated by his sudden death. "I could not believe my ears as I kept listening to what I was told," Judy recalled when told of her son's death. "There is no pain like loosing a child. It hurt so bad." Unfortunately the hurt would not go away before tragedy would strike the Allisons again.

Just eleven months later (July 12, 1993), Davey was piloting his own helicopter en route to Talladega (Ala.) Superspeedway to watch a friend, David Bonnett, in a practice session for an upcoming event. Apparently, Davey lost control of the aircraft, and it crashed in the track's infield. Longtime family friend (and David's father) Neil Bonnett made the call to his friends to tell them of the terrible accident. Davey, a husband and a father of two children would die the next morning of injuries sustained in the accident. Bobby and Judy again faced the unspeakable. "It was tough. I literally felt Clifford and Davey leave my body. It was tough. The pain was so bad that I cannot even describe what I felt," said Judy.

The stress and agony of everything the couple had been through drove a wedge into the marriage and eventually led to divorce in 1997. "We could no longer deal with each other's pain. We had to be apart," Judy admitted. "Bobby could not deal with me and I could not deal with him."

Apart they stayed for several years until their paths crossed again at a fellow racer's funeral. Kyle and Pattie Petty lost their oldest child, Adam, in a racing accident, in May 2000 at New Hampshire International Speedway. Bobby and Judy decided to come together to support their grieving friends. What they did not realize is that their love for each other was still there, and from that point on they did not leave each other's side. They remarried on July 3, 2000.

Bobby and Judy now reside in Charlotte, N.C., where they enjoy visiting their friends in racing and making an occasional trip to the track. Judy admits that a day does not go by that she does not think of her two sons and that sometimes "it gets real tough."

"The most important thing is that Bobby and I can deal with each other now and help each other instead of hurt each other," she said. "We are so lucky to be back together after everything we've been through. Racing will always be a big part of our lives, but it's not the only thing in our lives like it used to be."

Bonnie married James "Bubba" Farr, in 1992, has four children and resides in Hueytown, in the house where she grew up. Carrie married — in 1999 — and she and her husband, Scott Hewitt, live in Charlotte.

BOBBY ALLISON

A little known fact about Robert Arthur Allison: Before he could legally drive on the street he was practicing spinouts in a field. He entered his first race while a high school senior, finishing 10th, but after a couple of spills, his dad, Edmund, made him quit. The teenager got around the order, however, by competing under the name "Bob Sunderman."

Bobby Allison was born Dec. 3, 1937 in Miami, Fla., but because he relocated north to the "Heart of Dixie" in the early 1960s, he's been known to most racing fans as an Alabamian. At the height of his popularity, he was acknowledged as the leader of the "Alabama Gang," a group of racers including himself, his younger brother, Donnie, Charles "Red" Farmer and later on, Neil Bonnett.

After relocating to Hueytown, a suburb of Birmingham, Allison's racing efforts intensified and he won the NASCAR Modified-Special Division championship in 1962-63. He also tested the waters in NASCAR Winston Cup racing, in 1961, running four events in his own equipment.

Four years later, he made eight NASCAR Winston Cup starts, finishing in the top 10 three times, and in 1966 he ran 34 of the 49 races on the schedule. He broke into the winner's column for the first time on July 12 when he won a 300-lapper at Oxford Plains (Maine) Speedway. He won twice more, at Islip, N.Y., four days later, and on August 24 at Beltsville (Md.) Speedway. His win in Maine was Chevrolet's first series victory since Wendell Scott won at Jacksonville, Fla., in December 1963.

Allison began picking up rides with leading teams, as well as running for himself, and became a consistent winner on the circuit until his career ended in 1988. He was especially potent on the superspeedways, winning 10 races at Dover, Del., the Southern 500 four times, and the Winston 500 at Talladega, five times. After several "near misses," he won the 1983 NASCAR Winston Cup championship on the strength of 25 top-10 finishes in 30 starts, including six wins.

Allison's final victory was his third Daytona 500 win, in 1988. On June 19, he was involved in a horrendous crash at Pocono, Pa., that almost ended his life. He recovered, though, and is still one of the sport's most popular figures.

NANCY ANDRETTI

*N*ancy Summers and John Andretti went to the same high school in Indianapolis some 21 years ago. Even though they were acquainted, it was a year after they graduated before the couple had their first date. "I was dating someone else in high school, so I wasn't really looking for a date," Nancy recalled. John and I knew each other, but we didn't see each other that much because we didn't run in the same circles – and he was always racing."

After graduation, John left for Bethlehem, Pa., to attend Moravian College (where he graduated with a bachelor's degree in business administration), while Nancy remained in Indianapolis and got a job in a department store. He came back home the following summer, called Nancy and asked if he could take her out. "I was seeing someone else, and we broke up. John convinced me to go out with him. I wasn't completely sure about it but went anyway," she said. "Our date was awful. John had taken me to this French restaurant that was real stiff. I had to wear a dress, which I did not like at all. I think he was trying to impress me. I was not impressed and thought to myself I would not do this again."

John must have had a different opinion of their first time out together because he called her for another date ... and he kept calling ... and calling. "My Mother said, 'You have to go out with this guy so he will stop calling.' She told me to do something so he would stop." Somehow, John was able to get Nancy to go out with him again, and to her surprise her feelings toward him started to change. "I realized I did like him more than I thought. I don't know really what happened to make things different."

John continued living in Pennsylvania while in school but came back to Indy every weekend to race. Nancy, who was not a race fan, started going with John on her days off. "I did not grow up around racing so it was all new to me. Racing was so big in his family which was so different from what I was used to."

The miles in between the two and the separation got to be too much for the young couple so Nancy moved to Pennsylvania to live with John's grandparents while he lived with his Uncle Mario (Andretti) and shared a room with his cousin, Michael. "It didn't really mean that much to me that Mario was so well known. It was no big deal because to John they were family."

In 1986, Nancy went with John to an IMSA sports car race in northern California. The two went out for the evening, and John suggested they check out the Golden Gate Bridge. Unbeknownst to Nancy, he thought one of the most popular attractions in the

(Left) The Andrettis had an unusual courtship, but thanks to John's persistence, the relationship culminated in marriage in 1987. (Opposite page) An Andretti family portrait: While Amelia (in John's arms) seems to be wondering about what's going on, Nancy, Olivia and Jarett are obviously enjoying themselves.

As busy as he is, John managed to find enough time off to take his brood on a short ocean-side vacation to South Carolina, in 2001. They all consider Renita Rhine (left of Nancy) to be a member of the family.

country was the ideal spot to propose marriage. Unfortunately, all parking areas were closed at night. "I didn't know what he was doing," Nancy said. "He was so upset. He just said I didn't understand. We drove down to the bottom of the bridge where he found a park. He pulled out the ring and asked me to marry him. I didn't know it but he wanted to propose in the middle of the bridge.

"We took our children back there and showed them where we got engaged. It was special to show them the park."

Nancy and John were married, in 1987, in the Roman Catholic Church in Indianapolis where she had gone since childhood. They started their family a few years later with the birth of their first child, Jarett, on Dec. 13, 1992, about 10 months before John ran his first Winston Cup Series race. When Jarett was a year old Nancy became quite ill, and doctors found she was intolerant to gluten, (the medical term is "Celiac Sprue"), which is found in wheat-flour products. It wasn't a particularly easy time for the Andrettis, as they were also moving to the Charlotte area to be closer to Winston Cup racing.

"I was really sick," Nancy recalled. "My condition caused muscle atrophy and I had lost a lot of weight. My body was stripped of the nutrients it needed. That was a stressful time for us." Luckily the doctors were able to properly diagnose her and get her on a road to good health. On March 29, 1995, John and Nancy celebrated the birth of their daughter Olivia, while Amelia Lois (named after Nancy's mother) entered the world on May 10, 2000.

Although John was the 1982 stock car rookie of the year at Dorney Park Speedway in Allentown, Pa., and at one time even successfully tried his hand at NHRA Top Fuel drag racing, he came from a family famous for its exploits in open-wheel competition. John himself had won in Midgets, Sprints and even Indy Cars, so when he set his sights on the Winston Cup Series, Nancy had mixed emotions about the transition. "That was a little tough for me because I loved my friends in the Indy series, but I knew it was the best move for John at the time," she said. "The schedule for the Indy Cars was not as bad as the Cup schedule, either. I was nervous about the move for John and for me."

Nancy and John made the transition well, though, and Nancy started making new acquaintances in the NASCAR community. One of her best friends quickly came to be Kim Burton, with whom she is still very close. "I don't know how people do it without friends – especially when you have kids because they just gravitate toward other kids," she said. "Like Olivia and Paige (Jeff and Kim Burton's daughter) … they are attached at the hip. They are best friends so Kim and I are around each other because of them, too. Kim and I travel together when we can, which makes it nice."

Nancy feels she must be at the track when John is racing and tries hard to balance her time between the kids and her husband's career. She admitted, though, at times her life can be overwhelming. "It's hard sometimes because the kids miss a lot by being gone all the time," she said. "John misses the normal parenting stuff like going to soccer games. I have a wonderful girl who moved with us from Indiana, Renita, and she helps me with the children. She gives me peace of mind knowing that she is watching the kids when I can't. She is like a member of our family."

One of the biggest losses of Nancy's life was the passing of her mom, Lois Summers (far left) in 1998. From left: sisters Susan Blackwell and Jane Devore; Nancy; sister Ann Faires and Nancy's grandmother, Edna Brochin.

(Right) When John decided on a NASCAR career, Nancy had reservations about leaving open-wheel racing. But she knew it was for the best.

(Below) Proud Papa Carl Summers and his offspring: Ann Faires (top left) and Jane Devore; Nancy and (bottom right) Susan Blackwell.

(Opposite page) John's dad, Aldo, also put aside a tradition of open-wheel racing to help his son adjust to stock car racing life. Motorsports has been a family passion for decades.

Nancy had always been very close to her mom, Lois Summers. After John's Winston Cup career was in full swing, she found out her mother had been diagnosed with gall-bladder cancer that had spread to her liver. "That was the worst time for me," she said. "I had always been so close to her. We were living in Charlotte, in 1998, while she was still in Indianapolis, so I couldn't be there with her like I wanted when she was so sick. I didn't like to miss a race because I felt I needed to be with John. I did miss a Bristol race that year to be with her. That was a hard time for my family and me. I was so torn."

In November '98 Nancy's seven brothers and sisters called. They knew their mother was approaching the end of her life. "They called me to tell me to come home so I did. It was one of the hardest things I ever had to do," Nancy said. "I was the only one with her when she died. I was so devastated by her death.

JOHN ANDRETTI

NASCAR racing's "Renaissance Man," John Andretti was born March 12, 1963 in Bethlehem, Pa., calls Indianapolis his "home town" and lives in Mooresville, N.C., which is just a short distance from his "office" — Petty Enterprises in Randleman.

If anyone was "born to race" it was probably Andretti. His uncle is Mario Andretti (no explanation needed), his dad is involved in the sport, his cousin, Michael, is an accomplished competitor and his godfather is A.J. Foyt (again, no explanation necessary).

Andretti began open-wheel racing at age 16 when he went overseas to attend a driving school. At 19, racing at the old Dorney Park Speedway in Allentown, Pa., he was named the stock car division rookie of the year. He switched to USAC Midgets in 1983 and was that division's top rookie.

He made his Indy Car debut with CART in 1987, finishing sixth at Elkhart Lake, Wis., and won the Australian Gold Coast Grand Prix in 1991, the same year he finished fifth in the Indianapolis 500 and made the semifinals in his first shot at NHRA Top Fuel drag racing. Two years before — 1989 — he won in his class in the 24 Hours of Daytona.

In 1993, Andretti broke with the family's open-wheel tradition and decided to "settle" in on the Winston Cup circuit. His first start came in October 1993 at North Wilkesboro, N.C., for Hagan Racing. He ran three more times that year and in 18 races for Hagan in 1994 before switching to Petty Enterprises for the rest of the year. Prior to the change, he became the first driver to run both the Indianapolis 500 and Coca-Cola 600 Winston Cup race on the same day.

He left the Pettys at the end of the year and joined a Ford team owned by Michael Kranefuss. Andretti's '95 season was mediocre, so after 22 races in 1996, he and Jeremy Mayfield swapped rides. Andretti went to Cale Yarborough Motorsports and Mayfield joined Kranefuss.

Although Andretti won his first Winston Cup race while with Yarborough — the 1997 Pepsi 400 at Daytona Beach, Fla. — he was unsatisfied and "came home" to Petty in 1998.

Andretti has run 262 Winston Cup races through 2001, with two wins, four poles and about $11,600,000 in winnings to his credit.

"When you lose your mom it is a tragic thing because your whole life revolves around her. I still think about her all the time and it still hurts. I'm sure that it will always be that way. Having babies and my mother's death are the two things in my life that have really made an impact on me and my life."

John and Nancy live on a lake in the Charlotte area but are looking to build elsewhere. With the busy racing schedule, they don't have much time to spend on the water and would also like more privacy. Nancy's interests are gardening, cooking, tennis and photographing her children. She squeezes these activities into her life when it's possible but knows at present her husband's career comes first.

John's been driving for Petty Enterprises since 1998 and said he has found a home there. He plans on racing for quite awhile before quitting for good. "I don't know what we'll do when he retires," Nancy said. "I wouldn't mind maybe moving back to Indy one day. It depends on how rooted the kids are in Charlotte. I wouldn't even mind if John did something else other than racing. Racing is what we do — and it has been good to us — but I don't want to go racing when I am 80."

DIANE BODINE

*D*iane Dallaire was just 20 years old in 1980, when she set out with her identical twin sister, Donna, and five of her girlfriends for a five-hour road trip from Seekonk, Mass., to Long Pond, Pa. Their ultimate destination was a Modified Division special event at Pocono Raceway. She didn't know it, but an informal chat with an auto racing journalist would change her life.

"I had been going to races all my life so I was a big fan of the sport," Diane explained. "I had a lot of friends there in Pocono. I was talking to one, Bones Bourcier, who worked for a racing publication. Brett walked up and asked Bones to introduce us. Brett and I talked for a few minutes; then I walked off. Brett followed me and we talked for about an hour. It was getting late and we still had to drive five hours to get back home. My sister and girlfriends were very upset with me. I finally left with the girls.

"We pulled up at a gas station to fill the car up and Brett pulled up right beside us. It was like 2 am at this point. He walked up to the window and when he did, my sister said in a not so nice way for Brett to take me or get away from the car because she had to go to work. My sister was really mad. I climbed in the car with him without even really knowing him. It sounds crazy, I know. The funny thing was we went to McDonald's to get something to eat. When he was going to order, I said, 'Get me a drink; anything but diet.' He got me the biggest diet drink they had," she said with a laugh. "I should have known right there to get out of the car."

Brett was about 21 and was living in a trailer in Dallas, Pa., a small town between Scranton and Wilkes-Barre. He spent many nights making the five-hour trip to Massachusetts to see Diane, and she reciprocated to be with the guy she had fallen in love with. "I don't know what it was with us but we just knew we were supposed to be together," she said. "We got tired of the traveling back and forth and decided to get married. We got married just four months after we met. It was January 11, 1981. My grandfather thought I was crazy. He would always say that Brett should get a real job instead of just going round and round."

Diane moved to Dallas to be with Brett where they shared their small trailer with some extra cargo. The little mobile home was part of his "package." It was rent free, provided by his Modified car owner, and he also got $125 a week and a portion of his winnings.

"My girlfriend, Carol Araujo, was so upset about me moving away that she and her little girl went with me," Diane said. "Brett's crew chief, Lance Klass, and his girlfriend also lived with us in this three-bedroom trailer. There was no insulation in the trailer, and we

(Left) Heidi Bodine was born into the sport and has always been one of her father's biggest supporters and biggest inspirations. (Opposite page) Brett and Diane's closeness has always been a source of strength for both.

(Above) The Bodines are not just a couple but also a team. They both own and run the NASCAR Winston Cup team and share equally in all aspects of the business.

(Right) Brett and his younger brother, Todd (right), here with Brett's nephew Josh Richeson, have always been close, even when times have been tough for both.

lived in the Poconos. Brett would go outside with a blow dryer and thaw out the pipes. Snow would blow under our door. We had the best time in that trailer."

Brett and Diane stayed in the infamous trailer for a year before moving with their daughter, Heidi, to Connecticut to race. "Brett was following his dream to race, so I knew we had to go. I didn't mind that much because I loved racing, too. It turned out to be a great thing for us. We met some of our dearest friends, like Anne and Clyde McLeod, who we are still very close to.

Clyde was Brett's crew chief. We stayed there for four years. Brett won the Modified Race of Champions in 1985, which was great. It was the biggest race of the year."

In November 1984 with young Heidi in tow, Brett and Diane moved south. Brett went to work on Rick Hendrick's NASCAR Winston Cup team where his older brother, Geoff, was the driver and Harry Hyde was the crew chief. Thanks to his brother's misfortune,

Brett got his big break in March 1985. Geoff, who was also racing NASCAR Busch Series cars for Hendrick, crashed at Bristol, Tenn. He was scheduled to run the NASCAR Winston Cup car the next weekend and therefore couldn't make the Sportsman event race at Martinsville, Va.

"Geoff convinced Rick to allow Brett to drive the car at Martinsville. Rick said if he could repair it, he could drive it," Diane said. "So, Brett fixed the wrecked Bristol car, went to Martinsville and won. It was unbelievable. Brett ended up running 13 races for Rick that year. Out of the 13 we won three, had three poles and finished 10 times in the top 10. It was an amazing year. I would take Heidi and go to all the races. I didn't want to miss anything."

One of Diane's very special memories came at the 1987 NASCAR Busch Series awards banquet the year after Brett went NASCAR Busch racing full time. "It was tough for us when we moved south because we were from the Modifieds up north. We were not liked very much by a lot of people," she remembered. "Sometimes people could be really cruel to us. We were attending the NASCAR Busch banquet when they announced the Most Popular Driver award for that year. To our surprise they said it was Brett. We couldn't believe it after all the animosity the year before. It was a real special honor for Brett and me."

When things go well at the track, Diane isn't shy about letting everyone know it. After Brett made a good qualifying run at Lowe's Motor Speedway, it was time to celebrate.

Brett's career blossomed from there. He ran his first NASCAR Winston Cup race in 1986 for Hendrick, 14 more the next year for team owner Harold "Hoss" Ellington and jumped into the series full time in 1988, driving Fords for Bud Moore.

"It was a good time for us," Diane said. "Heidi was in school, which made it a little more difficult at times because there were things at school that she wanted to do that either Brett and I couldn't be there for or she missed to be at the track. She did make friends at the track growing up, though. Heidi was around the same age as Dale Earnhardt, Jr., Adam Petty, Justin Labonte and a lot of other kids so it made things easier for her having friends at the track."

Diane and Brett suffered through a very difficult year in 1993 when Brett lost his good friends, Alan Kulwicki and Davey Allison. Kulwicki, the 1992 NASCAR Winston Cup champion, died in a plane crash in April. Allison perished in July when the helicopter he was piloting crashed at Talladega (Ala.) Superspeedway. "When you're in this business you have a lot of friends, but when you lose someone as close to you as Davey was to us, it's so hard to get over it," she said. "It was such a hard time for both of us. We were friends with both Alan and Davey, but Davey was one of Brett's closest friends. It was hard to stay focused during that time. If it had not been for our family and friends, I don't know what we would have done."

As if the year had not been hard enough, in September Brett was in a serious accident at Dover, Del., during race qualifying. "It was a violent wreck. He knocked the wall back 10 feet," Diane recalled. "He literally knocked the wall down. He had a 'bleeder' on the brain and a broken wrist. He had surgery that following Wednesday and raced that weekend. He never missed a race. I can't believe now I let him do that. It was really stupid. I was so ready for that year to be over. My heart could not take anymore."

In 1995 after many years driving for someone else, Brett and Diane had an opportunity come along that had been for so long just a dream for the couple. After driving for legendary team owner Junior Johnson for one season, Johnson announced he was retiring and wanted to sell the team. He offered it to Brett and Diane. "We had always wanted our own team," she said. "Brett called home one day and said, 'Diane, we have to do this. If we don't, someone else will." We found out how much he wanted and said, 'no way!' We could not afford it."

After lengthy negotiations, the couple worked out an agreement with Johnson and assumed ownership in 1996. They put everything they had – financially and emotionally — on the table to fulfill their dream. "We knew it would not be easy, but we were willing to give it a try," she said. "We had gotten burned so many times along the way but found ways to get around some of the high costs. Our biggest problem, of course, is money to support the team year in and year out. Ownership has it pitfalls, like the constant stress Brett and I are under to keep it going every year. It's great owning our own team. It's just the pressure these days is so incredibly intense that it is hard to completely enjoy it."

Keeping the team afloat remains more than ever a problem, and one that's not taken lightly by the Bodines. The lifeblood of any racing operation is sponsorship. Without corporate monetary aid, it's almost impossible to remain in business. Brett Bodine Racing began the 2002 season with just agreements with "associate" sponsors but had no prime backer.

"We certainly can't do it on our own. Getting a ride for Brett with another team isn't the answer, either, because you can lose a ride as fast as you can lose a sponsor," Diane admitted. "I don't know the answer to our future except it is in God's hands. We would like to bring along Josh (their nephew) to race for us when Brett retires. We are looking for ways to stay in the sport after Brett retires and still make a living. Racing is more stressful now. The demands are more on everyone involved. I sometimes ask myself if it is worth it but always come back to the same thing: This is all we know to do."

BRETT BODINE

Born on Jan. 11, 1959 in Elmira, N.Y., Brett Bodine is 10 years younger than brother Geoffrey and five years older than his other sibling, Todd. All three were exposed to racing at an early age through their father, the late Eli Bodine, who owned a short track in Chemung, N.Y.

The "middle Bodine" started at the bottom by competing at Chemung Speedrome in the Hobby Stock Division in 1977, the year he got out of high school. He went on to graduate, with honors from the State University of New York with a two-year degree in mechanical engineering, began running NASCAR-type Modified Cars in 1980 and won the prestigious Race of Champions for Modifieds, in 1985, at Pocono, Pa.

Bodine's next step in an expanding career was his debut in the NASCAR Busch Series in 1985. Driving for car owner Robert Gee of Harrisburg, N.C., he entered 13 races and won three. The following year, he finished second in the race for the series championship, just 20 points behind champion Larry Pearson. He was named the series' Most Popular Driver in 1987 and in all won 16 poles and five races.

Bodine ran his first NASCAR Winston Cup Series race in 1986 for team owner Rick Hendrick. He started 32nd in the Coca-Cola 600 at Lowe's Motor Speedway and finished 18th.

Bodine ran 14 NASCAR Winston Cup Series races in '87 for the part-time Ellington Racing team of Wilmington, N.C., finishing seven. He committed himself to the circuit in 1988, signing on with Bud Moore Engineering of Spartanburg, S.C. In 1990, he moved to Kenny Bernstein's team and won the spring race at North Wilkesboro, N.C. His association with the team owner/NHRA drag racer ended after five years when he joined the Junior Johnson and Associates operation in 1995.

It was a pivotal season in racing, as Johnson announced his retirement from the sport, winding up a career that began in the 1950s. Bodine and his wife, Diane, purchased Johnson's team and Brett Bodine Racing made its debut in 1996.

LYNN BODINE

Lynn Brown was no fan of the Bodine brothers. Her father, Charlie, was a friend of NASCAR Modified champion Richie Evans and they were well acquainted with the Bodine family. She knew enough to know she would never consider going out with any of them — until a remarkable night in Thompson, Conn. The evening would forever shatter all her preconceived notions of anyone named Bodine.

It was at the Thompson Speedway dinner and dance in 1984 that the two had their fateful meeting. Lynn was 19 years old and Todd was 20. They were on the packed dance floor when suddenly they started dancing with each other. Lynn knew she liked this guy but knew nothing about him except his first name — Todd. It wasn't until the next day at the speedway that Lynn discovered the horrible truth. This was a Bodine! The fact that she actually danced with the "enemy" wouldn't sit too well with her friend, Richie, who had a continuing "thing" going with Todd's oldest brother, Geoff, although he was, by now, an established NASCAR Winston Cup Series driver.

Todd was apparently interested and asked Lynn out for lunch the next day. Lynn, being young and hardheaded, decided she liked him and accepted the invitation — no matter what anyone said. Even though Todd was working for Bob Sharpe Racing, in Connecticut, and as a fabricator on movie star Paul Newman's road racing cars, he still did not have enough money to pay for lunch. Lynn laughs at the idea of him asking her to lunch when she had to pay for it. "It was pretty funny but I had been around racing enough to know what the guys made and it was not a whole lot," she said.

Todd and Lynn made plans to meet at Pocono (Pa.) Raceway that weekend, where Geoff was racing. There, Lynn met someone who would become very dear to her, Diane Bodine, the wife of Todd's other brother, Brett. "They had been married for several years when I met her. That was so long ago but I can still remember it well," Lynn said.

Lynn was in college and Todd was working at any job he could find in racing. In 1985, Todd relocated to North Carolina to be closer to the center of NASCAR racing. He moved into a mobile home and found a job at Hendrick Motorsports, for whom Geoff drove. Todd and Lynn continued to see each other and would date for three years before they decided to make it official. They were married on Nov. 13, 1987 in Harrisburg, N.C. Lynn then moved south and made the trailer her home as well.

(Left) The Bodine family finds that there is life outside of NASCAR stock car racing. They took some time off to pose with a "friend" at Disney World a few years ago. (Opposite Page) Lynn hopes for some good "racing luck" as she watches Todd compete.

(Right) Daughter Ashlyn added a new dimension to Lynn's life when she came along in May 1998. The Bodines moved into a new home at about the time of Ashlyn's birth.

(Below) Even when he doesn't win, a driver has to go through the post-race interview — so it's nice to have your wife by your side for moral support!

Todd started running a limited number of NASCAR Sportsman Division races and set his sights on the NASCAR Busch Series. Lynn was helping Todd with his racing as much as possible but admitted life was a struggle. "It was hard to get things going then because he did not have much experience," she said. "We just worked hard to get things going and keep them going." Lynn also served as Todd's spotter on race day. "I learned so much about racing while I was spotting for Todd. It taught me about racing itself and helped me to respect racing overall."

In her travels with Todd, Lynn made a new friend. Andrea Blackard was the girlfriend of another young driver, Joe Nemechek, who was also trying to advance his career. Lynn and Andrea hit it off immediately. What attracted her to Andrea? "It was her vibrant personality," Lynn said. "She just has a way of drawing people to her."

Andrea would later become Joe's life mate, which allowed the young women to work their way through the ranks together as fledgling racing wives. "Andrea and I have been through a lot and when you do that you become even closer," Lynn explained. "She knows what I'm thinking and I know what she's thinking without even saying a word. It's important in this sport to have someone who knows what you're going through and who will always be there for you, and that is what I have in Andrea." The two would go on to share many happy

moments together, including a day Todd and Lynn had dreamed of for a long time.

Todd's first major win came in a NASCAR Busch Series race at Dover, Del., in 1991. Davey Allison and Ernie Irvan both ran out of gas on the last lap allowing Todd to make that first trip into the winner's circle. There was, however, one glitch. Todd was ill and couldn't even talk. Lynn did the entire post-race interview and even remembered to thank the sponsors. "We had waited so long for that moment," she said. "There was no way that I could let it go by without thanking everyone who had helped to make it happen along the way. It was pretty funny, though, that I had to do it."

Todd and Lynn's hard work paid off when Todd landed a 10-race NASCAR Winston Cup deal in 1994 with team owner Butch Mock. The ride would last through 1995. It was what the couple had worked so hard on together for so long, and it was finally happening. Racing was again a "family affair" with brothers Geoff and Brett also competing on the circuit. "There

(Above and left) Lynn is an accomplished equestrian, who keeps, raises, shows and rides horses in competitive events. It's a hobby that gives her a break from auto racing and it's a love she also can share with her daughter.

(Above) Lynn enjoys a lighter moment with Davey Allison, who perished in an aircraft accident in 1993.

(Right) Lynn and Todd believe that God sent their daughter to them at just the right time. Their daughter complements their life and has brought joy into it.

(Opposite page) One of the perks of being in racing is being able to enjoy the good times together. This includes the enjoyment derived from winning an event.

were always a lot of Bodines around. They were everywhere," she said, remembering some of her most special times as a member of the clan she once regarded with suspicion. "Todd was running 15th with 20 laps to go in the 1995 Winston Open. He flew past the field and won the race. That was great because we were at home with our friends and family to celebrate with us."

Todd still struggled, though, as he was trying to make his mark in the sport. Also, Todd and Lynn decided it was time to build a new house and start a family, never thinking it would be something that would take years to accomplish. They purchased some land outside of Charlotte and began building their dream home in 1997, a project that would take two years to complete.

After several years of trying to have children, the couple turned to a fertility expert for help. "It was a tough time for both of us. We continued to race but our minds would slip away sometimes," Lynn said. "Todd was being so strong. I did well, but sometimes it would just get to me." After six years of trying to have a baby — with a very aggressive fertility program — Lynn became pregnant with their first child. Ashlyn was born in May 1998. The room was filled with the couple's dear friends, as they wanted to share in the miracle of bringing a precious baby to the world. "Todd and I believe that God picked the exact time for us to have Ashlyn because of everything going on in our lives," she said. "He knew when was right for us." Todd and Lynn brought baby Ashlyn into their newly completed home. Attached to their dream house was a barn for Lynn's horses.

Lynn, always a fiercely independent woman, enjoys things outside of racing. One is a devotion to horses and riding. She loves to ride and to show her horses, a hobby she now shares with her daughter. "I feel that Ashlyn needs something else in her life besides racing, so she and I go to about one horse show a month," she said. "I love racing, but I have to have a break from it sometimes. I need something that is mine ... separate from Todd ... and that's what my riding is for me."

Lynn also shares the love of horses with another dear friend, Renee Cope, the wife of 1990 Daytona 500 winner, Derrike Cope. Both are avid riders. They obviously became friends through racing but love to ride together or just get together to talk horses while the guys talk cars.

Fear of injury, or worse, has not been a big factor for Lynn, even though she has seen a lot of bad racing mishaps over the years. She believes the sudden death of her 27-year-old brother, Charley, in 1983 from the injuries he sustained in an automobile accident prepared her for her life in the sport. It was a difficult experience for her, but one that made her strong. She learned that racing is only as nerve-racking as you allow it to be. "I try to be careful, especially now with Ashlyn, about getting too stressed. Children pick up on the stress so I try to control my thoughts and my actions while I am around her or other kids," said Lynn.

Todd and Lynn are involved in several charities, among them the YMCA, Brain Injury Association and Make-A-Wish Foundation. Lynn has been a staunch supporter of the NASCAR Winston Cup Racing Wives Auxiliary for many years and has also served as an officer. Todd and Lynn are also very

supportive of the Motor Racing Outreach, a ministry for racers and their families. Lynn is quite open about her faith and how it plays a role in her life as a wife and mother. "I lost a brother and three cousins, who were all about my brother's age. That made me turn to God and have faith," she said. "I also found out how strong I am. I feel that helps me now as I teach Ashlyn about God and help her to build her faith. My faith is very important to me."

Lynn and Todd have begun to plan their future because they both realize he, at age 38, can't race cars forever. They figure he's got about 10 more years as an effective competitor.

"We will probably own a NASCAR Busch team and Todd might possibly do some consulting, but that won't be the only thing," Lynn said. "Todd is a graphic designer. He does all his paint schemes and his driving suits, so I can see him doing something with that, in addition to the racing business. But racing is something that is just a part of you. When you live this racing life as long as Todd and I have, you just have to realize it will always be that way."

TODD BODINE

Todd Bodine's career in NASCAR Winston Cup Series racing has had some high spots but there have been a few frustrating times, too. Fortunately, the youngest of the Bodine brothers is a highly talented competitor who has found quite a bit of success on the NASCAR Busch Series circuit.

Bodine ran his first NASCAR Winston Cup race in 1992 for Donlavey Racing of Richmond, Va., and the next year began a three-season, 68-race stint with team owner Butch Mock. What appeared to be a promising association ended when Bodine left and returned to the NASCAR Busch Series. He did, however, in 1996, run 10 NASCAR Winston Cup races for three car owners.

The following year he ran five NASCAR Winston Cup races for as many team owners, and in '98, landed what looked like a great ride with a new team and a national sponsor, a pepper sauce. That enterprise caved in a third of the way through the year in what was called the "Tabasco Fiasco," and Bodine ran seven more races for another car owner. He ran the same number of events in '99, five in 2000 and then landed a full-time ride with Haas-Carter Motorsports and sponsor Kmart in 2001, replacing the retired Darrell Waltrip.

A disappointing season carried over into 2002. Kmart Corp. went into bankruptcy early in the year, ended its association with the team and Bodine was out of a NASCAR Winston Cup ride after just four races. He did, however, win the pole for the 400-mile race at Las Vegas, and this no doubt helped him land a NASCAR Busch Series ride with Herzog-Jackson Motorsports in mid-March.

Bodine was born on Feb. 27, 1964 in Chemung, N.Y., and grew up working around his dad's race track, Chemung Speedrome. He started racing Modifieds in 1983 and after moving to North Carolina raced Late Models, competed in the old NASCAR Sportman Series, worked at the Buck Baker Driving School and for teams owned by Bobby Hillin and Billy Standridge.

Between 1986-2001 Bodine ran 252 NASCAR Busch Series races. He started on the pole six times, went to victory lane on 13 occasions and has won almost $1 million.

SUSAN BONNETT

S usan McAdams was a 17-year-old Alabama girl when she was set up on a blind date, in 1963, with a boy from Ensley High School in Birmingham. Susan's best friend, Diane, was dating a guy named Bill, who just happened to be this boy's best friend. Bill did not have a car, but his buddy did, so he decided to set Susan up so he and Diane could have a car and go out on Friday night.

Susan's date was Neil Bonnett.

The foursome went to see *The Pit and The Pendulum*, a Vincent Price horror movie playing at a drive-in theater. Neil and Susan hit it off immediately. "It was an instant thing between us. I am not sure why; it just was," Susan recalled.

Susan was attending West End High School while Neil was at Ensley, both in the Birmingham area. While not schoolmates, the two still managed to see each other quite often. "Neil was very quiet and shy and I was the complete opposite," said Susan about their different personalities.

Susan knew from the beginning that Neil had a love for cars and especially racing. As neither had much money they found things to do that wouldn't cost a lot. They would go out every Sunday afternoon and sit on a hill, where they got a clear shot of turn four at Birmingham International Raceway, a 5/8-mile asphalt oval at the state fairgrounds. Susan remembered Neil's face as he saw the cars go around. "He loved to go watch the cars at BIR. He was so infatuated with them and their speeds. I know he always wanted to do that by the look on his face."

Neil and Susan continued to get more serious about their relationship. Even with both being just 17 years old, they decided to get married. They didn't tell a single soul of their plans to become husband and wife. They hopped in their car one morning and headed to Chamblee, Ga., an Atlanta suburb, to find a justice of the peace before anyone could talk them out of it. When they arrived at the JP's home they found they were not the only people with wedding plans that day. The daughter of the justice himself was getting married and the house was full of people. "There were people everywhere. They called us into their home and married us anyway. It was hilarious; there we were in their house with a big wedding going on and it was not ours," Susan said of their wedding day.

Neil and Susan then turned around and drove home. They decided not to tell anyone about what they'd done just hours earlier. Susan was frightened of how her dad would react, thinking he

(Left) Neil, his face covered with the grime of 188 hard laps, enjoys Talladega Superspeedway's victory lane with Susan after winning the 1980 Talladega 500. (Opposite page) Twelve years later, the couple were guests at the International Motorsports Hall of Fame induction ceremonies, also at Talladega. Neil was inducted posthumously in 2001.

David Bonnett (right) was 25 and his sister, Kristen, was 16, when David got married in July 1989. David pondered a career in racing but relinquished the idea because of family responsibilities of his own.

"would either kill me or have a heart attack." Neil was working as a bag boy in a grocery store, but that would not be enough to calm Susan's father's worries, so she thought. They hid the marriage license and kept it a secret from everyone. When they arrived home later that day there was snow up to their knees. They were lucky to make it back with the weather as bad as it was. "All I kept thinking is if we do not make it back home in time, our families will kill us," said Susan. Neil dropped his new wife at her house and then he went home. The newlyweds would come up with a plan to tell their families — but just not that day.

When neither she nor Neil could stand the secrecy anymore, or the separation from each other, they decided to tell her mother first, then the rest of the family. After the news was broken to everyone, the newlyweds finally moved under one roof. They got an apartment not too far from their parents. Neil started working full time at the grocery to help support what was about to be a family of three. Neil and Susan were expecting their first child.

Susan remembered an incident one night in the small apartment that quite possibly became a good reason to find a new home. "Neil was out of town and a tornado was headed right for our apartment. I was pregnant and pretty big at that point. I had to get under the bed to protect myself from possible harm. When the storm passed I could not get out from under the bed. My neighbors got worried and came looking for me. They had to lift the bed off of me because I couldn't get out. That's when I said, 'I am not living here anymore,'" she said with a grin.

Neil still wanted to race, but his biggest problem was money. He didn't have the necessary financing, so he did the next best thing — continue to dream. The young husband, however, figured out how to support his family financially and even have some money left over to save so that one day he could compete. He enrolled in a school that would train him to be a pipe fitter. It was an excellent plan, but one that took five years to complete.

Neil finally graduated and did quite well working at construction sites around Birmingham. Susan remembered his days as a pipe fitter all too well. "He was doing really good at his work, but he decided that sitting up on high beams was not the job for him. He hated that. He desperately wanted to race and was set on making it happen." Neil started hanging out in every race shop he could find; one in particular was that of Bobby Allison in nearby Hueytown.

Neil started helping Bobby out with his NASCAR Winston Cup Grand National cars and for his labor, in turn, picked up valuable knowledge. Eventually, he drove Bobby's short-track sedans at BIR where all his dreams started years before sitting on that hill on Sunday afternoons with his girlfriend, Susan.

"Bobby and Neil had a special friendship," said Susan. "They were good friends. Judy (Bobby's wife) and I became close, too, because they were always together." The bond between the two men deepened to a point that when Neil drove a souped-up illegal car through Hueytown and was arrested, it was Bobby — not Susan — who he called to come get him out of jail. Neil was afraid his wife wouldn't be too pleased with his choice of street cars. "You just never knew what Neil was going to get in to. He always kept me wondering," she said.

As Neil's racing career was taking off, Susan was busy at home taking care of two children. Their firstborn, David, and their daughter, Kristin, kept Susan from being able to go to the races as much as she would have liked. She felt the constant stress of trying to be a mom to her children and a wife to her husband, who was now on the road all the time living out his dream. When she did make it to a race, she would travel with Neil in the tow truck because they did not have the money to fly. Like the other women at the tracks, she had to keep her children in the infield because neither she nor the kids were allowed anywhere near the cars.

Those who knew Neil well were aware of his infectious laugh and his devilish character. "You never knew what Neil would do," said Susan. She remembered one Yuletide season in particular where he pulled a particularly good prank on her. "We had decided not to buy each other anything for Christmas. When Christmas morning came along there was a big package under the tree for me from him. I told him he wasn't supposed to do that. When I opened this beautiful package there were jumper cables in it.

He said I needed some!"

Another year stood out in her mind. Their anniversary was just a few days before Christmas. Neil gave her a beautiful diamond ring for the first occasion, and just a few weeks later on Christmas Day, he gave her another diamond ring.

Neil competed on weekly short tracks for many years to gain the skill to race at the NASCAR Winston Cup Series level. David and Kristin were getting old enough that Susan

Neil, Donnie Allison (center) and his older brother, Bobby, donned white tuxedos for this publicity photo touting them as the "Alabama Gang." Only Bonnett was born in the state; the Allisons "emigrated" from Florida in the 1960s.

41

In the early 1990s, retired NASCAR Winston Cup champion Bobby Allison (left) and Dale Earnhardt, the reigning champ, were guests on Neil's popular television program, "Winners." He was enjoying his second career as a broadcaster at the time of his death.

could take occasional trips with her husband. This was a time in which they both were truly enjoying their lives and each other.

Living was good for the couple until April 1, 1990 during the TranSouth 500 NASCAR Winston Cup race at Darlington (S.C.) Raceway. Neil was swept into an accident not of his making that left him with a temporary loss of memory and put him in a nearby medical facility for several days. He was then transferred to a hospital in Birmingham to recover.

"Neil had been in many accidents over the years so I thought it would all be fine," Susan said. "His amnesia created a whole different set of circumstances from what we had dealt with in previous accidents."

The healing process was long and hard, and even though others lost hope of Neil's return to racing, his desire to compete never was in doubt. During this time, though, a new opportunity knocked. Neil made the transition from driver to broadcaster as he used his knowledge of the sport and his driving experience to become a race analyst for TNN, the "Nashville Network." He also had his own show on TNN, *Winners*. "I was not surprised by Neil being successful at both because I thought he could do whatever he put his mind to doing," noted Susan.

This career change marked a big turning point in Neil and Susan's lives, one that carried with it many struggles. "It was so different not having Neil race," she said. "Everything changed ... my friends changed ... Neil and I had to start over ... make new friendships and new relationships. It was a difficult time, especially for me, because Neil was busy working, and I felt like I was on the outside looking in."

As Neil was enjoying his success as a TV personality, David was now showing interest in racing himself. The mere thought of her son becoming a race driver created mixed emotions in Susan. "I did not want to alter his feelings one way or the other. Neil and I had always been serious about not making the kids feel that they needed to stay in racing, as they became adults themselves. However, I did understand this desire because I felt it was imbedded in both of them," she said.

David did take up the sport and was participating in a practice session at the massive Talladega (Ala.) Superspeedway in July 1993 with his dad there to offer advice. Davey Allison, the son of Bobby and Judy, who himself had a successful career going in NASCAR Winston Cup racing, also made plans to spend the day at the track with his longtime family friends.

Piloting a helicopter, Davey approached the track's infield and attempted to land. Something went terribly wrong and he suddenly crashed. It was Neil who pulled Davey's broken body from the wreckage. Neil and Susan would stay with the Allisons all night until the devastating news the next morning that Davey had succumbed to his injuries. "That nearly killed Neil," said Susan. "His heart broke when he made the call to Bobby and Judy to tell them of the horrible accident. We both loved Davey like our own. Neither one of us ever forgot that day."

Life went on for Neil and Susan as they struggled to get over their close friend's death. Susan threw herself in to helping Bobby and Judy deal with their long emotional recovery and Neil found solace from another dear friend, Dale Earnhardt. The two racers were very close, quickly became the best of friends, and Susan recalled their special bond. "Neil and

Dale liked all the same things. They both loved to hunt and fish. They were two peas in a pod. They were both very funny men. They were clowns."

Of one of the many trips that Neil and Susan took to North Carolina to visit Dale and his wife, Teresa, Susan recalled a story of "kitchen-humor," which also illustrated a side of Dale unknown to many. "Neil was out working on a car in Dale's shop and Teresa had gone to take their daughter, Taylor, to dance class. Dale and I were hungry so we fixed dinner. He actually prepared most everything. Then everyone in their family came over to eat with us. It was a nice dinner, and everything was served on their best china." Susan laughed when she said things were not the same when Teresa and Dale would come to their house for a visit, noting, "They would eat off of whatever we could find."

Neil never lost the will to get back in the driver's seat and Susan still struggled with his desire. "I did not want to urge him to race again because I felt there were so many other things he was better at," she said. "It would be Dale that would enable that dream to become a reality. Neil would go along with Dale to his practice sessions and occasionally hop in the driver's seat. I was not surprised because I don't think in his mind he ever completely gave it up."

Neil made a "comeback" of sorts in 1993 and ran two NASCAR Winston Cup races, finishing out of the top 10 in both. It, however, was just enough to rekindle the desire in Neil to restart his driving career. It was Speedweeks in Daytona, 1994. Neil had decided to run the Daytona 500 in a car owned by longtime friend James Finch. Susan could not leave for the Daytona trip as early as Neil did so she chose to make the drive on this particular day with her friend, Edith Bracknell. She left instructions with David and Kristin back home how to get in touch with her in case of an emergency, not ever thinking one would arise as she was making the eight-hour drive from Alabama to Daytona Beach, Fla.

Neil was in the midst of a practice run at Daytona when he lost control of his car. He slammed the wall with such force that he never regained consciousness and was pronounced dead on arrival at the hospital. The call had to be made to Susan to let her know of the tragedy. She was told of Neil's accident by Motor Racing Outreach chaplain Max Helton via cell phone while she was somewhere outside of Jacksonville, Fla. She still had a couple more hours to travel, now knowing that her husband would not be there to greet her. "That was the longest drive I have ever taken. If it had not been for Edith, I don't know what I would have done. I can hardly remember anything about that day," she said.

It took Susan several years to deal with the death of her husband. She missed her friends in racing, but she learned to detach from the things that brought her down. "We had so many plans which we didn't get to do. We really wanted to travel to places where we had never been before," she said.

Susan has made a new life for herself now at her church where she has a very supportive "family." She enjoys playing the piano and hopes to write music one day. She has spent time teaching adults to read and also enjoys cooking. Her thrill everyday is looking in to the eyes of her grandchildren. "I look back and thank God for bringing me through that time in my life," she said. "There were some great times but there were also some really bad times, too. I remember thinking, on occasion, 'Please let this be over.'"

David Bonnett has since relinquished his dream to become a race driver and has chosen to be home with his own family, his wife, Tracy, and their two children.

Daughter Kristin is single and living in Hueytown near her mom.

In April 2001, Susan made a rare appearance to accept on behalf of Neil, his induction into the International Motorsports Hall of Fame in Talladega. There, she radiated a glow of peace as she shared funny anecdotes with her many friends. For instance, she once sent Neil out to get food for their dog. He loaded up his four-legged pal in his truck and away they went. When Neil returned home without the dog food Susan asked where it was. Neil responded: "I took him through the McDonalds drive-through!"

NEIL BONNETT

Lawrence Neil Bonnett began a NASCAR Winston Cup Series career — that included 18 victories and almost $4 million in money won — at Talladega, Ala., in 1974 and basically ended it there about 20 years later.

Born in Hueytown, Ala., on July 30, 1946, he got his early racing experience on the short tracks of his home state, basically at the fairgrounds oval in Birmingham. He entered his first NASCAR Winston Cup race in 1974, the May 5 Winston 500 at Talladega (Ala.) Superspeedway, in a 1972 Chevrolet, where he started 33rd and finished 45th. He returned to the 2.66-mile trioval that August in a Chevy owned by his mentor, Bobby Allison. He qualified 26th fastest but finished 39th because of engine failure.

Over the next two years, he raced 15 times in his own equipment and then got his first major-league ride with the famed No. 77 K&K Insurance Dodge. But team owner Nord Krauskopf closed it up after just 11 races and Bonnett signed on with a new owner, Kentuckian Jim Stacy. His first win came that September at Richmond, Va., and he won again at Ontario, Calif., in November, the last race of the year.

Bonnett ran all of 1978 with Stacy, winning once, a partial season in '79 with three owners; 1980-82 for the Wood Brothers; 1983 with RahMoc Racing; 1984-86 with Junior Johnson; 87-88 with Rahmoc; 1989 and into 1990 with the Woods. After a crash at Charlotte in October '87, where he fractured a hip, Bonnett returned to win the second and third races of the '88 season. He also raced on a new superspeedway in Australia that year and beat his mentor, Allison, for the win.

Bonnett's career effectively came to a close in the fifth race of 1990, the TranSouth 500 at Darlington, S.C., where he was involved in a vicious crash not of his making. While his physical injuries seemed minimal, Bonnett ended up with severe amnesia. He recovered, spent about four years in television broadcasting, made an unsuccessful "comeback" at Talladega in July 1993, ran one more race that year and died on Feb. 11, 1994 while running practice laps for the Daytona 500.

KIM BURTON

*F*ourteen-year-old Kimberle Browne was out for an afternoon bicycle ride on Main Street in South Boston, Va., when a car pulled up beside her with two boys inside. One of them yelled something to her trying to get her attention.

Young Jeff Burton was the kid on the passenger side of the car. He was not soon to forget the face he saw that day and fully intended to find out who was on the bike. Even at the age of 15, he knew he was smitten.

It wouldn't take him long to find out who the mysterious girl was. Not long after, he was talking to a friend and mentioned the girl he had seen and his quest to find out who she was. He was thrilled to find out that not only did his friend know who the girl was but he also had her phone number. His buddy had gone to kindergarten with Kim and had known her for most of his life.

Jeff called Kim and the two ended up talking for hours. They also made plans to meet at a football game that weekend. She and some of her friends went in a group to the stadium to meet Jeff, who had a reputation of being "cool." Hence, the girls were quite surprised to meet a guy who appeared to be fairly normal. And no wonder. Jeff was on his bicycle. He rode up looking cool, called out Kim's name and said he was the guy who had called her. Suddenly, he realized he had no brakes on his bike. As he was waving, he plowed right into her and her friends. Kim thought that the whole ordeal was quite amusing. "He was trying to be 'Mr. Cool' when he rode up on his bike. When he crashed, you could not even tell he was embarrassed. He just hopped up and kept talking like nothing was wrong."

Kim wasn't totally amused with this kid but she did know one thing — he was persistent. Kim's reaction to their first encounter: "He was a crazy fool and I couldn't believe him."

Love, however, can be mysterious. Jeff continued to call Kim and they'd talk for hours. They'd sometimes meet at the at the movies on weekends but only after telling their parents they were seeing their friends and not each other. Her father did not like Kim and Jeff spending so much time with each other. He felt they were too young, and besides, this was the first time his young daughter had shown such an interest in anyone. Of course, Kim had a different opinion of the relationship.

Kim and Jeff went together for some time before they broke up in high school. Jeff was catching a lot of flack from his friends about

(Left) Kim and Jeff exchanged wedding vows in a church not too far from where they both grew up. The ceremony was solemn — unlike the reception that followed! (Opposite page) Harrison was a few days past his first birthday when he joined Mom and Dad in victory circle at Phoenix.

(Above) Kim and Kimberle, at age 4, enjoy Jeff's NASCAR Busch Series victory at Rockingham, N.C., in early 1999. It was his only win on the circuit that year.

(Right) One of Jeff's biggest victories in his career as a NASCAR racer came at Darlington, S.C., in September 1999 when he won the Pepsi Southern 500. Anyone who wins at "The Track Too Tough To Tame" has really accomplished something.

the time he spent with Kim so he decided to end their relationship. Even though they had "broken up" they had lunch together every day in the cafeteria. Kim planned her rebellion carefully as she would write the names of other boys on her notebook to make Jeff jealous. The ploy worked. They had been apart just three months when Jeff said they should just get back together because they loved each other anyway, so why not? Kim agreed with his logic and was thrilled with picking up the relationship.

Kim and Jeff had been sweethearts for a long time but there was still a side of him that she did not know. Jeff was racing Go-Karts on the weekends when they were not together. One weekend in particular, Kim was at the beach with her family when she got a call from Jeff, who told her he'd been in a race that night and had won. He was at the track helping a buddy work on a Street Stock car when his friend had a little trouble with track officials and was suspended. Jeff then got in the car, ran the race and took the checkered flag. She had no clue what he was even talking about. They had never discussed this activity of his and she didn't understand his intense interest. She knew he sometimes went to the race track but never thought he was interested in racing himself.

Kim soon found out that, like it or not, racing was to become a big part of their lives together. She started going to the races with him but he'd never let her in the pits because she was way too nervous. He'd been in an accident one night and she screamed and went to pieces, so he put a stop to that early on. She would sit with Jeff's older brother, Brian, and his friends while Jeff raced.

Kim and Jeff graduated from high school and started planning their future. "I kind of always knew we would get married. I just did not know when that would be," she said. "We

talked about it sometimes and I think it was always in the back of our minds," said Kim, who went on to college to become a teacher. "I did not know where Jeff's racing would go so it was always important to me to have something to fall back on, which for me was my education."

Kim earned her degree in math and science education and found a job teaching algebra in a nearby school so she could still be close to Jeff.

During this time Kim was still living at home with her parents. Jeff had found a house he wanted to buy for him and Kim to live in one day. The only problem was he did not have the money to put down on it. Kim took her life savings and presented the money to Jeff to use for a down payment. Kim's father, being very protective, was upset that she had given her life savings to her boyfriend, who was soon to become her fiancé; they just didn't know it yet.

Kim knew that she and Jeff were facing a decision about their future together. "We were just to the point where we needed to do something. Jeff had seen some marriages very close to

This formal family portrait is one of Kim's favorites. It was taken before the birth of Harrison in October 2000.

him deteriorate so he was scared that marriage might change our relationship. I found out later that Jeff had the engagement ring for a year before he got up enough nerve to give it to me. I still don't know what he was scared of. It was not like he had not known me long enough."

Jeff and Kim went out on what she thought was going to be a normal date but Jeff was acting oddly. He picked her up and they rode around in his car for several hours. Every time they'd stop somewhere, he'd talk about off-the-wall things and they'd go somewhere else. This went on for several hours until Kim suggested they return to his house. When they arrived, Kim, frustrated over the evening's events, told Jeff she was going home.

"I was so mad and frustrated. I could not believe how he was acting. As I was ready to leave, Jeff said, 'Could you do me a favor?'" Kim, already short nerved, said no. "He then nervously said, 'Would you marry me?'"

Kim and Jeff were married at the Main Street United Methodist Church, in South Boston, just a few blocks from where they met as kids. They exchanged vows on February 1, 1992 in front of friends and family and had, exactly as planned, a boisterous reception at the National Guard Armory. There was a band and everyone cut loose, including the ushers, who slid across the floor in their rented tuxedos. Jeff and Kim were responsible for paying for the damaged formal wear but decided the fun they all had was worth it. The couple honeymooned in

Cancun, Mexico, and then settled into the racing life.

Jeff was running in the NASCAR Busch Series while Kim was still teaching school. After her last class on Friday, she'd drive to wherever the race might be. Sometimes, to be back at work on Monday the return trip would take all night. This went on for three years; Kim was supporting the family and needed to work. It wasn't until Jeff got his first NASCAR Winston Cup Series ride in 1994 with the now-defunct Stavola Brothers team that she quit her job. "I wanted to experience the whole racing thing with him," she said. "We didn't know how long it would last so we decided to do it together. It was hard to leave my students, though."

Kim traveled with Jeff every weekend to be by his side. They also moved into a larger home in South Boston to welcome the birth of their first child, Kimberle Paige, who was born in July 1995. "She was such a great joy and still is for us," Kim noted. "It made things a little different from a travel standpoint but we adjusted well."

The Burtons' motorhome driver started bringing his wife along to tend to the baby while Kim joined the team on pit road. Kim is still one of the few "working" wives in the pits on race day. She keeps lap charts and monitors things like tire wear and fuel consumption. "I've always done this for Jeff since we started racing together," she said. "It makes me feel better knowing I have firsthand knowledge of what's going on with my husband. I also feel I have some control over things because I always know the situation. I'm afraid if I ever stopped I might get disconnected — and I don't want that."

The Burtons are no strangers to race-track safety issues. Even before NASCAR started mandating changes, Kim and Jeff were already

Jeff Burton was just a kid, somewhere between 5-7 years old when he decided racing Go-Karts looked like fun. His inspiration was his brother, Ward, who was six years his senior and already a racer.

Jeff Burton, born on June 29, 1967 in South Boston, Va., switched to hobby-type stock cars at South Boston Speedway in 1984 after winning two Virginia state karting championships and finishing second in points four times. He won six Late Model races at South Boston in 1986 and seven NASCAR Late Model Stock Car events there in '88, the same year he made his first of five NASCAR Busch Series starts. He was a full-time competitor on that circuit through 1993, and also made one NASCAR Winston Cup Series start.

In 1994, Burton made his official debut in NASCAR Winston Cup racing with the Stavola Brothers team. He recorded three top-10 finishes, was 24th in points and took the rookie of the year award. Burton spent one more year with the Stavolas before Jack Roush brought him into his ever-growing Ford stable of teams in 1996.

Burton scored his first NASCAR Winston Cup victory at Texas Motor Speedway in the spring of 1997, also won races at Loudon, N.H., and Martinsville, Va., and finished fourth in points. He won twice in 1998, recorded a season-high six wins in 1999 and won six more races in the next two seasons for a total of 17 trips to victory lane in 259 starts.

Burton has also remained active in the NASCAR Busch Series. He's averaged about a dozen starts a year between 1997-2001 and has 15 career wins and eight pole victories.

discovering things on their own. "I've always been a little fearful of racing, but it does make me feel good knowing that Jeff is so educated in that area. We've used our own money for crash-testing and other development projects. I'm extremely proud of Jeff for his dedication to safety. It relieves me to know as much as I do because of Jeff's work on and off the track."

Between the time Jeff joined Roush Racing in 1996 and the birth of son Harrison in 2000, the Burtons moved to suburban Huntersville, N.C., north of Charlotte. Kim now stays at home during the week, while Paige is in school, and catches up with Jeff on Friday evening. She and her good friend, Nancy Andretti, try to fly together to the tracks when their husbands must leave in advance. "We do that when we can. Our kids get along great and she is a dear friend of mine, so it allows us to be together — and it is fun," said Kim.

Jeff and Kim are in the process of building a new home on 60 acres in Huntersville, complete with a barn and horses for Paige. Kim is also involved in a business venture where she is a part owner of a new company, Pro Sports Management, which handles racing accounts and television personalities. "I got into it with a good friend, George Harris, who Jeff and I met in racing," she said. "I have really enjoyed my work and feel as the kids get older I'll become even more involved."

Kim realizes after Jeff retires in 10 years or so things will be quite different. "I cannot imagine us not staying busy because I am not a homebody. I like to go and so does Jeff," she said. "We don't know what to do when we do get a weekend off. We like juggling our lives. We are committed to this sport. It's just what we do. We would like to do some traveling together, maybe to Europe. We'd also like to get on a boat and cruise the Intercoastal Waterway and see many different towns."

Jeff and Kim celebrated their 10th wedding anniversary this year. Their secret to a successful marriage, according to Kim is being "focused on the same things. We set goals and make them happen together. It is amazing that after all the changes we've been through that we still love each other and are still focused on the same things. We've had the best relationship and are so blessed."

TABITHA BURTON

orn on June 8, 1967, Tabitha Throckmorton grew up in Scottsburg, Va., a small rural community outside of South Boston. Hers was a childhood where family was all-important. Most of her kinfolk were in Scottsburg. "We were all very close to each other; very family oriented, even now," she said matter-of-factly.

Tabitha graduated from Halifax County High School in 1985 and went to work in a plastics manufacturing plant. She later attended Southside Virginia Community College where she studied human services. When Tabitha was 20, in August 1987, she was dating a fellow, who had a buddy from South Boston, who raced stock cars. His name was Ward Burton.

"One night we went to the track where Ward was racing Late Models. We went in the pits to see him. I instantly liked him," Tabitha related. "Everybody liked Ward because he really is a kind person. I had never been to a race before so it was a different experience for me. I didn't really care for it that much at first.

"I didn't see Ward for awhile after that. I finally ran in to him one night in a restaurant. I was hanging out with some friends when he walked in the door. I walked over to say hello because it had been some time since I had seen him. We got to talking and after that we all kind of went out in groups. We didn't go out on our own for awhile. We went as a bunch of friends. I guess it was during that time that we really started to like being around each other."

Something clicked and Tabitha and Ward "got pretty serious, pretty quick." Their dates usually consisted of her going to the race shop to watch him work on his car. He was still a part-time racer with a full-time job at his dad's construction company. "I'd take him to dinner on Friday nights just so I could be there with him, or sometimes we would go out to dinner, but not often because we didn't have any money," she said. "Ward took a loan out one time to buy a welder — so we were pretty broke — and his paycheck always went into his racing. I was in school so I didn't have any money, either. He would always race on Saturday so the only time to really see each other was on Sunday."

Ward and Tabitha had a good idea of where their relationship was going, which was full steam ahead. "Ward and I always knew after we got together where we were going," she said. "We had talked about getting married but Ward was still a little scared of making that commitment. He had been through a family experi-

---

(Left) Tabitha and Ward were quite the dashing couple at the 2000 NASCAR Winston Cup Series Awards Ceremony in New York City. It was quite a step up from the short tracks of Virginia. (Opposite page) With Sarah and Jeb before the start of a race. Everett had yet to come "into the picture."

Tabitha and Sarah are a "team" of their own and do as much as they can together when time permits. Sarah is developing a life separate from racing and enjoys showing horses.

ence that made him aware of how hard divorce can be on everyone involved. I think he was scared because of that. After he finally got settled with the idea of marriage we just decided to get married. We just wanted a small ceremony with family and friends.

"We got married on January 26, 1990 at Beth Carr Baptist Church in Halifax, Va. We could not afford a large wedding. We even changed the date several times before we finally did it. We had a honeymoon a few years later in Saint Thomas (Virgin Islands)."

Ward's younger brother, Jeff, had been running in the NASCAR Busch Series for two years when Ward and his dad, in early 1990, were working on a deal to get him onto the circuit. Ward finally landed a ride with car owner Mike Swaim and ran 23 races that year. The same year, Tabitha graduated from community college and transferred to Mary Baldwin College in Staunton, Va., to further her education. She also went to work for The Halifax County Mental Health Center, in Halifax, as a crisis counselor where she worked in many different areas including substance abuse awareness and crisis

prevention. Tabitha was not only pursuing her chosen career, she was also trying to keep up with her husband's. After four full seasons in the NASCAR Busch Series, he made his first of 26 NASCAR Winston Cup Series starts, in 1994, for team owner A.G. Dillard.

"It was very busy for us then," Tabitha said. "We had two children by that point — Sarah and Jeb — and I was working. I would work all week, get off early on Friday and get the children and drive to the races. It wasn't like it is now with motorhomes and airplanes. I would sometimes leave the kids at home because for some reason Jeb hated to ride in a car. He would sometimes scream the whole time. It was incredibly hard and just not worth it at times to travel like that. In 1994 we did get a motorhome, which made things so much easier. My dad drove for us so it worked out good."

Tabitha and Ward built a small house in 1994 on her parents' farm in Scottsburg. The following year, they bought a house in a nearby neighborhood and in 2000 they built their home where they live now in Halifax.

(Left) Tabitha and the children are strong supporters of Ward's career and spend as much time as they can with him.

(Below) The pace of life for the Burtons really picked up speed when he joined the NASCAR Winston Cup circuit in the mid-1990s. During that period in their lives they moved twice, finally settling down in Halifax, Va.

The Burton's older son, Jeb, born in 1992, likes the "stick-and-ball" sports but has also taken an interest in his dad's occupation. Tabitha admits that she would rather he not take up racing when he comes of age.

As is the case with most racing wives, Tabitha splits her time between home and the track. The routine is easier for some women than it is for others — like Tabitha — who enjoys both facets of her life but finds the juggling act "really hard." She wants to participate in her husband's vocation and spend as much time as possible with her children.

"I've finally realized that I cannot be at two places at once so I have to pick and choose where I will be and what I can do," she said. "It's so hard to coordinate it all. Sarah shows horses. Jeb is active in football, soccer and basketball. The hardest part is when something happens on the track like the accident Ward had in California in April (2001). I was pregnant and at home when Ward wrecked out there. What makes this even harder is realizing drivers can and do get hurt sometimes when you aren't there. You just hope they are in the best of hands when you aren't.

"It scares me thinking that Jeb loves racing so much already. To be completely honest I would rather that he not race. I know he loves it, but it scares me. I do try to steer him in other directions. It is a little bit easier for us to keep Jeb away somewhat because there isn't a racing series around us for him to participate in. The thing about it is, he is good at it. It is a tough call. Fear is a funny thing for me because it multiplies with each accident. Ward was in an accident in 1994 at Charlotte where he got a concussion. After that I changed my feelings about racing. Now it seems to get worse, as I get older and the more that happens on the track. I try to trust in Ward and his comfort level. If he feels safe, then I guess I should, too."

Tabitha celebrated a personal landmark in 2000 when she graduated from Mary Baldwin after over ten years of college. She earned her bachelor's in Sociology. "I didn't do school the easy way. I had a family in between me trying to get my degree. It was hard at times but it was all worth it. To finally get my degree means a lot to me," she said.

On December 10, 2001, Ward and Tabitha welcomed a new precious baby, Ashton, into their family. Tabitha spent the last few months on bed rest as they anxiously awaited the birth of their third child. "It was hard because I'm used to going all the time but with the help of friends and family we made it," she said. "The toughest part was not being able to travel with Ward, but we are really enjoying Ashton so much. We're able to do so many things that we couldn't do when Sarah and Jeb were babies. We travel by airplane now and have a coach waiting on us when we get there. It is a lot of fun.

"I think when Ward retires I would just like to relax some. Racing makes our lives so restrictive, even though we love it. I would love to get out of the routine. If Jeb races, I'm sure we'll stay involved in the sport to help. If not, I don't know. Our family's future is an ever-evolving question."

WARD BURTON

Born on Oct. 25, 1961 in Danville, Va., Ward Burton may act and sound like he's just a "good ol' boy" — but in reality he's a fierce competitor with a variety of interests and a well-rounded education.

Burton, who resides in South Boston, Va., attended a military academy in lieu of high school, went to college for two years and spent two more living in a log cabin where he survived off the land by trapping, fishing and hunting for his food. After a lengthy racing apprenticeship, he also ended up as one of his younger brother Jeff's principal rivals on the NASCAR Winston Cup circuit.

At age 8, Burton began racing Go-Karts. When he turned 16, started competing in Mini-Stocks and Street Stocks at South Boston Speedway and in 1986 he moved up to NASCAR Late Model Stock Cars. This background paved his way into the NASCAR Busch Series, and in 1990 he drove in 23 races for car owner Mike Swaim and scored three finishes in the top 10.

Burton scored his first NASCAR Busch Series win in 1992 and collared three more the next year. That was good enough for his team owner, A.G. Dillard, to make the switch to NASCAR Winston Cup racing in 1994, where Burton ran 26 races with a best finish of second and a pole position at Lowe's Motor Speedway in October.

After 20 races in 1995, Dillard shuttered his team and Burton signed on with Bill Davis Racing, for whom he's raced since. Success was almost immediate, as Burton won his first NASCAR Winston Cup race — the AC Delco 500 at Rockingham, N.C., in October. Over the next four seasons, the team didn't win but consistently ran up front. In 1999, Burton recorded three second-place finishes at Rockingham, Darlington, S.C., and Las Vegas, losing each time to his brother.

Burton's second victory came in the spring 2000 race at Darlington, his third was the Southern 500, in 2001, also at Darlington, and he started the 2002 season off in fine form by winning the Daytona 500.

Burton also runs a wildlife foundation, which buys land in order to protect wildlife habitats.

CATHLEEN "K.K." CRAVEN

*C*athleen Grotton, today better known simply as *"K.K.," was born in Gardiner, Maine, in April 1969 and grew up just 20 miles south of what is now known as New Hampshire International Speedway. Even though her parents, Diane and James Grotton, and her uncle, Peter Prescott, owned and sponsored race teams through a family owned business, which her grandfather started, she did not consider herself a race fan. It would be a young, handsome speedster, who raced for her uncle on the American-Canadian Tour, a Late Model circuit, and was sponsored by her parents' water and sewer pipe distribution company, who would later capture her heart and cement her relationship with the sport.*

"I had just graduated from high school when I met Ricky for the first time. I was at my house with a friend, and Ricky was there to go have dinner with my parents. I was 18 years old and leaving for college in a week, so I was not really paying much attention to him because I had other things on my mind," recalled K.K. "I went off to college and came home in the fall to go to one of his races with my parents. I saw him there. After that my Mom would say, 'I saw Ricky today.' It wasn't until the following summer when I was home on break that I would actually go out with him.

"The race was at the old New Hampshire track before they totally changed it. It was a funny little track. They would stop the races there to let the ducks cross. When the race was over the entire team went out to dinner. I mentioned to Ricky about this great ice cream place in Manchester, where I went to high school. He rode with me there for milkshakes. It was a wholesome first date." She said with laughter. "I knew I liked him that night. I don't know what it was."

K.K. and Ricky hit it off that evening and started dating through the summer. He was living in Maine at the time, which was two and a half hours away. "We would meet on the weekends," she said. "We would drive back and forth. Once I returned to college in the fall the drive was a little better because I was on the coast, which made me closer to him. We were only an hour or so away from each other. Ricky was racing the American Canadian Tour (a short-track Late Model circuit that ran races in Canada and the United States) at the time, so many of those races were near me at school."

K.K., who was studying history and archeology at the University of New Hampshire in Durham, remembered working on papers in some pretty strange places — at noisy race tracks. "I learned to adjust to reading and writing from just about anywhere," she said. "People would ask how I could work with a loud race going on. As long as no one would talk to me I was OK. I am still that way today. I can read while things are going on all around me and it doesn't bother me."

K.K. and Ricky somehow knew they were the "real thing" and had talked about getting married, so it was not a huge surprise when Ricky proposed. There was only one problem: On the May night in 1989 when Ricky arrived at the university to see K.K. and take her out so he could "pop the question," she had way too much studying

---

(Left) Time spent together in Sept. 1989. Ricky and K.K. got married the following summer. (Opposite Page) K.K., Riley and Richard enjoy Tucson, Ariz., in November 2000. The Sonoran Desert certainly isn't like Maine!

(Above) K.K. and her family at a gathering in 1989.

(Right) Diane and James Grotton were at K.K.'s side when she graduated from the University of New Hampshire in 1991.

to do. "I lived in an all-girl dorm so I would sneak him in all the time. All my friends would help me," she said. "This particular night he asked where I wanted to go eat. He wanted something real nice. I told him that I was too busy and had too much work to do so we would have to go to D'Angelos (a sub shop). We went there even though it was not what he had planned. When we got back from dinner, there were roses waiting on me in my dorm room. He proposed right there."

One year later — June 29, 1990 — between her junior and senior year at the university, Ricky and K.K. were married. The ceremony was performed on campus. "We planned our wedding on a Friday night just in case a race was rescheduled — and it was — so we had to cancel our honeymoon and go to Monadnock (N.H.) Speedway. We ended up taking our honeymoon trip a few months later in January 1991, which was nice."

The two young newlyweds moved into an apartment in Dover, N.H. K.K. commuted to school during her final year, while Ricky worked out of a small shop in nearby Concord. K.K. graduated from college that following spring with a degree in history and a minor in archeology.

Ricky was running the NASCAR Busch North Series during this time. He had high

hopes of advancing into the NASCAR Busch Series, which would mean making a move south. K.K. was expecting their first child any day. On December 31, 1991 their daughter, Riley, was born. Four weeks later, the Cravens moved from Concord to Concord — New Hampshire to North Carolina! "I had a little baby and we had just moved into our house," K.K. said. "Ricky was racing with a team out of Danville, Va., at the time. I did not go much with Ricky then because it was so hard to travel with Riley. It was hard to keep a baby in the van all day. I potty-trained Riley at Dover Downs Speedway (the superspeedway in Delaware) because the bathrooms were so far. It was not fun."

K.K. split her time between the home they purchased in 1995 and the race track. Ricky was racing on the NASCAR Winston Cup circuit by this time so their fairly simple life became a bit more complicated. While K.K. was seven months pregnant with their second child, Ricky was in an accident at the Talladega (Ala.) Superspeedway.

"I had just been with Gina Pressley (driver Robert Pressley's wife) when Bill Elliott got hurt," she said. "I told her I don't know what I would do if that happened to Ricky. It was right after that when Ricky crashed. I was trying to get to the infield care center. I stopped along the way to try to see but no one would let me. Until your husband gets in a wreck, I don't think you realize how hard it is. Everything changed for me after that. It changed my whole perspective."

K.K. gave birth to their son, Everett, two months later on August 12, 1996, one day after the event at Watkins Glen, N.Y. K.K. and Ricky also built a cabin in the woods in Maine to have a

(Above Left) The future Mrs. Craven caught relaxing in summer 1974.

(Above Right) She enjoyed the warm weather in March 1985, too — in Cairo, Egypt!

(Below) The Cravens posed for the photographer at Martinsville (Va.) Speedway in October 2000 when Ricky ran for team owner Hal Hicks.

(Below) New Englanders at heart, the Cravens were able to spend a bit of "down time" at Moosehead Lake, Maine in July 1999.

(Opposite page) The same location a year later. Ricky and K.K. enjoy the calm and quiet of rural Maine, especially with their children.

place to get away from the demands of the racing circuit. "We love going to our cabin. It is a place that we can go hike and do all the things we love to do."

In 1998, Ricky sustained injuries from another accident at Texas Motor Speedway. "It was my birthday so Andrea Nemechek, Lynn Bodine, Gina Pressley and myself went shopping for the day. For some reason none of us had cell phones with us," recalled K.K. "When we got back to the track that afternoon, it was pouring down rain. We all said that practice must have been rained out. When we got to the gates I saw Ann Schrader waiting under an umbrella to let me know what had happened before the media got to me. She was such a big help as she explained everything that had happened. She explained that he was airlifted out and what his injuries were. She had been waiting on me for hours. That is what makes our friendships so special in racing. She wanted me to know before the press got to me."

Ricky fought hard to run well in the Hendrick Motorsports No. 25 Chevrolet and get back to some sort of normalcy after his two terrifying accidents, but fate would not have it, not at that point anyway. He won the pole for the first race of the year at New Hampshire but wasn't feeling well. He was diagnosed with post concussion syndrome and decided to turn over his ride to someone else.

"Ricky called Rick Hendrick and told him of his decision to step out of the car," K.K. said. "It was tough because he had a solid deal but he felt he could not take the risk just to stay in the car. He was one of the first drivers to step up and say, 'I can't do this; I won't do this to my

family or me.' I think he earned a lot of respect when he did that. That started out as one of the hardest times in my life. Ricky was miserable not racing. He had reconstructive leg surgery while he was out, which was hard on all of us. I had a one- and five-year-old and was driving Ricky everywhere. It was hard for me to understand his negative feelings. I wanted to say just get over it, you are still here. I am glad you are still here because his wrecks were so bad that it could have been different. But at the same time I tried desperately to understand. He was not a whole lot of fun to have around."

As Ricky worked hard to get back on solid ground, he, K.K. and the children began to focus more on their time together instead of him not racing. "Ricky got to enjoy so much with the kids like he never had before. We went to our cabin for the entire summer. It turned out to be such a blessing for us. It gave us both an awareness, especially Ricky, of what else is out there. There is more than just racing. Once he made the decision to go back racing we both realized we had to go back with a different angle, which we did."

Ricky did go back and after many years in the sport captured his first NASCAR Winston Cup victory at Martinsville, Va., in 2001. It was a win K.K. would miss. "I had been there all weekend, but when it was rained out I went home because the kids had school. I was so happy. I still would have liked to have been there, but you know you can't always be there no matter how hard you try."

The racing lifestyle can, at times, be chaotic. K.K. credits her survival in the sport with the friendships she's made. "My friends are so important to me. They are the only ones that can really understand all the emotions I feel, the disappointments, and the fears. Andrea (Nemechek), Lynn (Bodine) and Nancy (Andretti) have always been such good friends and so many others, too. It is just an understanding that we all have."

K.K. was close to earning a master's degree when she decided she didn't have anywhere to go with it. So she opted to get her teaching certificate in case she'd ever want to go back to work. She also loves to write and has authored several children's books that she hopes to have published one day.

Ricky is in the prime of his career but plans to retire in about 10 years. As K.K. put it, he has an interesting take on where life will lead him after racing.

"Ricky says that in 10 years he is going to drive my motorhome to archeological sites. He will cook while I dig," she laughed. "Until then I guess I'll screw up enough courage to go to the next race. I take it week by week. I just do it. That's how I live."

RICKY CRAVEN

A track announcer introducing "Richard Alan Craven" prior to a race would probably elicit a "who's that?" from the crowd. The more familiar "Ricky Craven" would, however, undoubtedly generate a lot of applause.

Born in Bangor, Maine on May 24, 1966, but calling Newburgh his hometown, Craven is one of the most well liked drivers in NASCAR Winston Cup Series racing. His stock rose considerably on Oct. 15, 2001 when he won the Old Dominion 500 at Martinsville (Va.) Speedway in Cal Wells' PPI Motorsports/Tide Ford. It was Craven's 174th career start.

Craven got his start in racing at age 15, running Late Models throughout the Northeast. He was a regular competitor on the American-Canadian Tour (ACT), a special-event Late Model circuit for two years (1987-89), joined the NASCAR Busch North Series in 1989, took Rookie of the Year in 1990 and the series title in 1991. Through 1999, he'd recorded 13 wins and an equal number of poles.

After 12 starts in the NASCAR Busch Series from 1986-91, he went full time on the circuit in 1992-94 and through 2000 had run 140 races with 57 top-10 finishes, including four victories. He also earned his second top-rookie title in '92.

Craven made one NASCAR Winston Cup Series start in 1991 and joined the circuit full time in 1995. Driving for team owner Larry Hedrick, he posted four finishes in the top 10 and was named the Raybestos Rookie of the Year. That made him just the second modern-era (1972 forward) driver to win rookie titles in three NASCAR divisions.

Craven ran one more year with Hedrick, joined Hendrick Motorsports in 1997, and finished third behind teammates Jeff Gordon and Terry Labonte in the Daytona 500. He missed two races because of injury but won the Winston Open non-points event in May and finished the year 19th in points.

The following four seasons were frustrating for Craven. He crashed in the fourth race of 1998 and was sidelined by post-concussion syndrome for much of the season. He ran four more races for Hendrick, resigned from the team and raced in the year's last three events for another operation. He raced just 40 times for two teams in 1999-2000 and then was hired by Wells.
In 2001, he finished in the top 10 24 times in 36 events and won almost $2 million.

CINDY ELLIOTT

*B*orn in Columbus, Ga., in 1965 but raised in North Carolina, Cindy Karam never thought when she accepted an offer to help a friend out one weekend as a photographer at a NASCAR Winston Cup event in Pennsylvania that she would, of all things, meet her future husband.

In July 1988 Cindy, a young studio photographer in Charlotte, N.C., who had never even seen a race before, got a phone call: Would she consider shooting a race at Pocono International Raceway? Her friend, Don Grassman, the photo editor of NASCAR Winston Cup Scene, a weekly racing newspaper, in nearby Concord, that covered only the NASCAR Winston Cup Series and closely related forms of the sport, needed help. He knew her professional background. They had worked together at the Northwest Florida Daily News in Fort Walton Beach, and although she had no experience with motorsports, Don felt she would do a great job.

"I knew nothing about racing before I got to Pocono," Cindy admitted. "I remember thinking that it was nothing like I expected. I thought it was a dirt track. I had no clue of what was going on. I called my dad that night to tell him it was asphalt.

"I was working the pits when Dale Earnhardt broke. They gave me this piece of paper that had the car numbers on it and where they were pitting. I was working with Steve Waid (one of the paper's editors) and Don that weekend. I told them if somebody would tell me Earnhardt's car number, I would cover the stop. I had no idea where to go. It was pretty funny now looking back."

It was this same race that Cindy would see Bill Elliott for the first time, but just in passing. In fact, she didn't have credentials to cover victory-lane festivities for the race winner — Elliott! It wasn't until a few months later that she would actually meet him. "I had to go to a pit crew championship party. It was an informal setting and everyone was just kind of chatting with each other. I ended up talking to him that night for awhile. I only knew his name was Bill and he was from Georgia. I thought he was a nice guy. I enjoyed talking to him," she said.

In 1989, Cindy accepted an offer to become a full-time staff photographer for WCS and an accompanying publication, NASCAR Winston Cup Illustrated magazine. She was covering the circuit on a regular basis. It was during this time that Cindy and Bill struck up an acquaintance. "We became friends. We just enjoyed each other, but

(Left) Bill and Cindy introduced son Chase to their favorite off-season activity — snow skiing and snowboarding in Vail, Colo. (Opposite page) One of Cindy's favorite portraits taken at the couple's wedding — chosen with the eye of a professional photographer!

it was no more than that at first," she said. "I was living in Charlotte and he was in north Georgia. He would come to Charlotte for different things and would eat at my house or just hang out. We were such good friends that he refused to eat my cooking. He would say, 'I'm ordering a pizza because your food looks so bad.'"

They remained good friends until a 1992 skiing excursion to Aspen, Colo., shook things up a bit. "We went skiing together, again as friends. It was on that trip that we realized we were interested in each other. It was a little weird at first but not for long. As Bill puts it, we were oil and water. We never thought we would be romantically involved." Cindy and Bill went on the trip as friends and came back as a couple. They started seriously dating each other but kept the new relationship under wraps. She was still working for the paper and magazine and thought a personal relationship with a driver might be construed as a conflict of interest. "Also, I was doing some more commercial jobs that I had been working hard on. I was not sure at that point where we were going, so we continued to keep it secret for awhile longer."

(Above) During the summer of '92, Bill and Cindy were dating steadily. Here, they were en route to an Elton John concert in Atlanta.

(Right) 1992, a tumultuous year for Cindy, ended on a high note when she and Bill were married in Blairsville, Ga.

(Left) Christmas 2000 was special for Bill, Cindy and a bemused Chase when Santa Claus — the Jolly Old Elf himself — arrived for a visit!

(Below) Cindy and Chase presented Bill with a dirt-track Late Model car in 2000 for Father's Day. About a year later, he drove it to a victory at Sugar Creek Raceway in north Georgia.

Cindy, who had always been very close to her dad, got the phone call she never dreamed she would get; not at this point in her life anyway. On September 7, 1992 her father, Thomas Karam, suffered a massive heart attack and passed away at age 59. "It was the worst news for me. I was so close to my dad," she said. "He had just had a complete physical and was told he was healthy. I couldn't believe he died. I still can't sometimes. His death left such a void in my life. It's funny. He always told me he didn't want me to marry a race car driver. The hardest thing for me now is when something happens, I want to tell him about it."

Cindy buried her father and struggled to get on with her life. Just a short time later Bill decided he wanted to spend the rest of his with Cindy — and didn't want to wait. "One night we were talking, and he told me he wanted to get married. I thought he was kidding and didn't say anything else about it," Cindy recalled. "The next morning he said he was serious about us getting married. It was somewhat of a shock." On Dec. 12, 1992, Cindy and Bill exchanged vows in Blairsville,

Ga. Cindy moved into a cabin that Bill had been living in on his property and knew right away the place would need a bit of updating. "In the spring of 1993 there was a big snowstorm. The snow was coming in the walls of the cabin through the cracks. That's when I said we have to remodel."

Cindy continued her photography for a short time after her marriage. She had always worked and had always loved putting images on film. Her father also appreciated the craft, and when she was growing up in New Bern, N.C., there was a darkroom in her house she and her dad both used.

"He taught me to develop my own film and how to look for and see the unusual, even in those things we look at in our own backyards every day," she said. "When I was in high school, I worked at The New Bern Sun Journal, and when I graduated from high school I was the only student

(Above) Keeping on eye on Bill while he races. Chase also listens in on the radio.

(Right) Victory lane at Homestead-Miami Speedway in November 2001. The Elliotts share the podium with car owner Ray Evernham (left), Ray's wife, Mary, and crew chief Mike Ford.

ever accepted at the Randolph Photography School based on my portfolio. My mother and father were very proud of that.

"But it got to be a little different with my working at the track and Bill racing," she admitted. "When he won the Atlanta NASCAR Winston Cup race in 1992 (Motorcraft 500 on March 15), I was in the photographer's pool taking victory lane pictures. He pulled me in with him and said, 'You need to be over here with me.' I didn't know what to do. I was used to being on the other side of the camera."

Cindy left NASCAR Winston Cup Scene shortly before it changed ownership at the end of 1992 and focused primarily on her impending marriage. She then settled into the routine of

being a top driver's spouse, and the couple celebrated the advent of their child, Chase, who was born on Nov. 28, 1995.

"It was a lot different for me traveling with Bill because we stayed in hotels then," Cindy recalled. "I would take warmers for the baby food. I remember when we got our bus; I didn't know how to run anything in it. I was scared of the whole bus idea. Bill wasn't there, and I turned on the microwave. It made some weird noises. Bill had to get me adjusted to the bus. I was not exactly sure. Of course I love it now, not having to deal with traffic and all the other things." Cindy and Bill spend their days away from the track either at their home in Georgia or their getaway in Vail, Colo. "We love Blairsville. This is where we will always stay. We also love snow skiing. We go several times a year. It is great to get a way from everything. It is something we all three love."

Chase, who, naturally, is still too young to be making career choices, has already mentioned he would like to race someday. Mom, however, is not sure that's' such a good idea. Yet, the youngest member of the clan already has a motorcycle, Go-Kart and a four-wheeler so ... "I would really prefer him not to race because it terrifies me. I look at what Kyle and Pattie Petty have been through (losing their son, Adam, in a racing accident) and I don't know how they do it. Chase says he wants to drive a race car. I guess we will have to see."

Bill, who is a lover of dirt-track racing, spends time on the red clay "bullrings" every chance he gets. Cindy and Chase gave him a dirt car for Father's Day 2000. A little over a year later, he ran a race at Sugar Creek Raceway, a 3/8-mile dirt track in Blue Ridge, Ga., and won it.

Approaching age 47, Bill is one of the older drivers on the NASCAR Winston Cup circuit. He and Cindy have discussed life after his career comes to a close, but they have come up with no clear plans for the future. "We had talked about owning our own team again (he was a car owner from 1995-2000), but things are so different now. I don't know if we want that pressure," Cindy said. "There are so many years between Bill and Chase that we will have to see what direction he goes. I think we will do some less complicated things ... like Bill playing around in his dirt car ... stuff like that. Bill is also very interested in land development, so who knows what that will lead to? I personally want to get back into photography. I'm doing more now than I used to but still not much. I do some things for some local people and friends. I really like personality portraits more now than what I did before I got married.

"I'm doing what I want now instead of what I have to do. I really enjoy it."

BILL ELLIOTT

The offspring of the late George and Mildred Elliott weren't the only racers to leave the confines of the mountains of north Georgia to ply their trade elsewhere, but in the annals of NASCAR they are undoubtedly the most well known.

While brothers Bill, Dan and Ernie were, in their early days as racers, truly a team, it was William C. Elliott — Bill — who captured the attention of the racing public because of his exploits of the 1980s. His accomplishments earned him the nicknames, "The Fastest Man Alive" and "Awesome Bill from Dawsonville." Although he went winless in NASCAR Winston Cup racing for six consecutive seasons, his popularity never abated. He was named by fans as NASCAR Winston Cup racing's Most Popular Driver 15 times, including 10 years in a row — a remarkable accomplishment for a low-profile personality.

Elliott was born on Oct. 8, 1955 in Cumming, Ga., but grew up in nearby Dawsonville. "Team Elliott" began competing on short tracks over 30 years ago. In February 1976, they brought a car to Rockingham, N.C., where Bill started 34th and finished 33rd. That was his first of 659 NASCAR Winston Cup starts — through 2001 — and he went on to win 41 times, corral 51 poles and earn over $27 million. In between, he won a record 11 superspeedway races (and poles) in 1985, the year he won the first "Winston Million" (three of four designated events with a $1 million bonus) and the championship three years later.

Michigan industrialist Harry Melling purchased the family's team in 1982, and the following year Elliott won his first race, in November, at Riverside, Calif. The association lasted through 1991 when Elliott left Melling Racing and drove for Junior Johnson from 1992-94, where he won six races. He formed his own team in 1995 but after six winless seasons, he closed it and joined Dodge and Ray Evernham Motorsports in 2001. There, he broke a winless streak of 227 races by winning at Homestead-Miami (Fla.) in November.

Elliott, in 1987, won eight poles, including the one for the Winston 500 at Talladega, Ala., with a speed of 212.809 mph. It's still the fastest qualifying lap in NASCAR Winston Cup history.

FRANCES FLOCK

It was sometime in 1941. She was a skinny 13-year-old girl dancing to a jukebox at the Pavilion in Atlanta when a stranger literally caught her off guard.

"I had gone to Grant Park with my girlfriend for a barbecue. Her parents let us walk up to the Pavilion to dance because they could see us from where they were. I started dancing the shag with this tall sailor who was about 6-foot-2. He slung me around and when he did, I lost my footing. This other boy I didn't know caught me. I turned around and the sailor was gone. The boy that caught me asked me to dance and I did. He then asked me to walk with him around the park. We walked around the lake and the beautiful Magnolia trees. We stopped walking and he leaned over and started kissing me. That was it for me. I felt it all over my body."

Frances Roberts got home that day — Labor Day — and told her mother and father about this stranger and how she had walked with him around the lake. "I told my parents not to worry because it was innocent and that I would never see him again. I didn't think I ever would, but I did think about him after that day."

Frances was too young to date so she spent a good bit of her time trying to slip around her parent's rules to go out with boys. "If I liked someone they had to come over and sit on the steps to talk to me. We could take walks around the neighborhood but that was it."

Frances didn't hear or see the boy, who'd saved her from falling down, for four months. Then, one day she got some unexpected company. "My same girlfriend that took me to the barbecue had a boyfriend, who had a friend that started calling me. I didn't have a phone so he would have to call my grandmother's. She would yell across the street, 'Frances it's some boy again.' I kept talking to him, not ever knowing it was the same boy I kissed under the Magnolia trees. One night we talked my mother into letting me go to the movies with my friends. When they came to pick me up, he got out of the car. I could have died. When he got out of that car, my heart went to my toenails. We went to the Fox Theatre to see *Springtime in the Rockies*. To this day, I still haven't seen it," she laughed.

That night, Frances, age 13, had "absolutely" fallen in love with Julius Timothy Flock, an Alabama native, who would find fame in racing simply as "Tim."

(Left) A "flock" of Flocks in victory lane after Tim won the 160-mile event on the 4.1-mile Beach & Road Course at Daytona on Feb. 27, 1955. He included his mother, Maudie, wife, Frances, and children Richard (left) and Donald. (Opposite page) Joy (left) and Peggy Flock joined Frances when Tim was posthumously inducted into the North Carolina Auto Racing Hall of Fame in 1999.

Frances and Tim's brother, Fonty, aren't shy about showing Tim how they felt after he won the Motor City 250 on the one-mile dirt track in Detroit June 29, 1952. The victory helped him cement the NASCAR Winston Cup championship that year.

Tim, then about 17, was working here and there while Frances was attending the eighth grade at a local school. One odd job in particular took him to her school everyday. "He was driving the delivery trucks for SunKist and would deliver drinks to our school cafeteria everyday. He would always leave me a cold drink. He was also a bellhop on Saturday nights. I would go down and stand on the road just to see him," Frances recalled. Tim left Atlanta for Texas and joined the Army as a military police officer. "My daddy was stationed in California in the Navy and Tim was stationed in Texas. It was just the normal thing during those times. Tim wrote to me the whole time he was gone. He was discharged after nine months because of bleeding ulcers. He came back home to Atlanta. I couldn't wait to see him. I was working in Rich's Department Store in the bridal salon when he got back. With my daddy being gone, I had to help my mother support the family so I couldn't go to school anymore."

Tim and Frances knew they were to be married. There was no question about it, but she had promised her father that she would wait until he got home from California. By then, however, Frances wasn't sure what was in store for her. Tim was having second thoughts about matrimony and was stalling for time

"I was working for Southern Bell at the time as an operator. I got home late one night and went to my room. About 20 minutes later I heard a tap at the door; it was Tim. He had on an old racing jacket and some nice slacks. I said, 'What are you doing here this late?' and he said, 'I have cold feet. If you want to marry me, it is going to be tonight or I am not getting married.' My mother came out of her room and I told her we were going to get married right then. She said Daddy would have a fit. I told her for the first time in my life I was going to defy her. She got dressed and went with us. We drove to Stockbridge, Ga., and knocked on the justice of the peace's door at 1:50 a.m. When we got there Tim realized he didn't have enough money to pay for our marriage license. I had just gotten paid, so I pulled out eight dollars. Tim joked that he paid that money back a thousand times to me during our life together!"

Following the nuptials on November 26, 1944, Tim moved in with Frances at her parents' house. The couple paid rent and remained there as new Flocks started coming into the world. Richard was born Aug. 31, 1945. Their second child, Ronny, was born the following April, two months premature, but died one hour later because of a heart-valve defect. Tim and Frances later moved into their own home outside of Atlanta in Stockbridge.

In 1947, Tim jumped at an opportunity to run a Modified car for North Carolina driver Alfred "Speedy" Thompson, at North Wilkesboro Speedway, which helped jump-start his career as a professional race driver. Frances was busy at home with their ever-growing family. Donald was born on May 13, 1947, and Peggy came along on Aug. 19, 1949. In 1950, Frances was six months pregnant when she grew concerned. She'd felt no movement inside her womb and delivered her stillborn daughter, whom they named Marie, in the back of their Cadillac on the way to the hospital. "I liked to have died when I miscarried Marie. I got real sick with blood poisoning. It was very scary, plus I was so upset about losing my baby," she said.

Frances and Tim would have two more children after Marie — Carl, born May 29, 1951, and Joy, Jan. 18, 1954. "Needless to say I didn't go to many races when the kids were all so young. I did go to Daytona in 1952 with a nanny to help with the children. It got harder though once the kids got up past third grade because they couldn't miss school," she said. "When I did go they would play in the infield with other racers' kids but it was really confining for the kids then."

Tim backed up his win at Daytona Beach in February 1955 by winning the race again a year later. His team owner, Carl Kiekhaefer, seems to be getting a kick out of the reaction of the winner's sons!

(Below) Tim drove a 1950 Oldsmobile 88 to victory in this event at Mobile, Ala. The unidentified U.S. Marine at the right won the Congressional Medal of Honor.

(Opposite page) Frances stays busy "looking after" her large family and honoring the memory of her late husband.

Tim was there for the birth of the National Association for Stock Car Auto Racing — NASCAR — in 1948. The following year, what today is called the NASCAR Winston Cup Series was formed, and Tim drove in five of the inaugural season's eight races. His NASCAR Winston Cup career was at its height in the mid-1950s and included two championships.

In 1959, Tim and Frances decided to sell their home in Atlanta and move to Miami so Tim could work in the import-export business. He'd battled bleeding ulcers most of his life and felt that his health was getting in the way of his racing. With a large family to support, he needed a steady income. The couple's plans for a life in South Florida were thwarted — literally at the last moment — by an ambitious race promoter with big plans. Olin Bruton Smith had teamed up with race driver Curtis Turner, and the partners were going to build a large race track just north of Charlotte.

"Bruton Smith knew what kind of station wagon we were driving on the way to Miami, so he called the highway patrol and had them literally pull us over to have Tim call Bruton on the phone," Frances recalled. "Tim called Bruton and sure enough he wanted Tim to come work for him at the speedway in Charlotte. Tim told Bruton we didn't have a place to live, and he said, 'I'll have you a place to live. Just come to Charlotte.' We turned the car around and drove to Charlotte. When we got there, he had rented us a house. Tim started working for the speedway, selling stock and whatever else they could find for him to do."

Tim ran his last race at Charlotte in 1961. At age 37, he felt he'd lost some of the edge needed to drive race cars at ever-increasing speeds. "It was hard for us to see his driving career end, but he felt that his reflexes weren't as good and he didn't want to drive like that," Frances said. "He wanted to retire as a champion, which I feel he did."

TIM FLOCK

Born in Fort Payne, Ala., on May 11, 1924 to Lee and Maudie Flock, Julius Timothy "Tim" Flock was one of a family of six children. His brothers Carl, Bob and Fontello (Fonty) and sister Ethel were older, while another sister, Reo, was the baby of the brood.

While Tim was still young, Carl joined their uncle, Peachtree Williams, in the bootlegging trade, and when Williams died, the family moved to Atlanta where Carl took over as head of the family business. While Bob and Fonty were also involved, Tim apparently was not. Instead, he went to work, holding jobs as a fireman, parking lot attendant and hotel bellhop.

Speed was in the family's blood. Lee raced a bicycle and owned the first car in Fort Payne. Carl was a boat racer, Reo an aerial daredevil, and Bob, Fonty, Tim and Ethel all raced stock cars and were NASCAR pioneers. In fact the three brothers participated in the first NASCAR Winston Cup Series race on June 19, 1949 at a dirt track in Charlotte, N.C. Fonty finished second, Tim fifth and Bob, who won the pole, was 32nd

It was Tim, though, who became most well known. His NASCAR Winston Cup Series record includes 40 victories in 189 races from 1949-62, a winning percentage of 21.2 that still stands. Additionally, he captured the series championship in 1952, winning eight races for car owner Ted Chester, in 33 starts. He took his second championship three years later, this time driving powerful Chryslers for Carl Kiekhaefer, the owner of Mercury Outboards (boat engines). It was his best season ever, with 18 wins in 39 starts and $33,750 in winnings.

Flock's final NASCAR Winston Cup season — just seven races — was cut short when NASCAR President Bill France Sr. banned him from the group "for life" because of involvement, with Curtis Turner, in attempting to unionize the drivers. France, however, rescinded the ban for both men in 1965.

Following his retirement, Flock was elected to eight halls of fame. Prior to his death on March 31, 1998, he was chosen by NASCAR as one of its 50 top drivers, while Sports Illustrated magazine, in 2000, chose him as the 11th Greatest Driver of the Century.

Though the ownership of Charlotte Motor Speedway had changed hands, Tim continued to work there many years. Frances got more involved with the track herself, as her children got older. "I would help Tim with the parade laps for the races. I continued on after his death because it is something that I love to do. I like to stay busy, I always have."

Tim, who had battled illness off and on through his life lost his final fight with lung cancer on March 31, 1998. His passing, naturally, was hard on Frances. It had ended a partnership of more than a half-century.

"He had not been feeling good for awhile. He would always tell me not to buy him anything like clothes because he wasn't going to be around the next year. Somehow he knew he was sick," Frances said. "I miss him. I miss his touch. I miss his companionship. We were always touching each other. I will always remember our dances together. We would dance sometimes three times a day. We would just stop and dance. I had the best husband for 53 years."

Frances spends her time these days with her five children, 10 grandchildren and beloved 92- year-old mother. She honors her husband's name through an annual golf tournament with funds going to the Ronald McDonald House. Tim has been inducted in to many halls of fame over the years, including the International Motorsports Hall of Fame in Talladega, Ala. In early 1998, just prior to his death, NASCAR named him one of its 50 top drivers of all time.

"Tim would always get real excited when he would find out about the different awards," Frances said. "One of the most special was when NASCAR announced him one of its 50. He was standing at the door waiting on me that day with the good news. If he was in the door when I got home, I knew he had something to tell me."

DeLana Harvick

*B*orn *in Winston-Salem, N.C., in July 1973, she was a young, energetic public relations representative when she met Kevin Harvick for the first time at driver introductions at Michigan International Speedway in July 1999. When a friend of hers said the young NASCAR Craftsman Truck Series driver would be the next superstar, DeLana took the prediction with the proverbial grain of salt. Her father, John Paul Lineville, was a racer and she'd been around racing all her life. So another "young gun" did not impress her. While she would meet the young Californian many times during the next few months, her opinion of him wouldn't budge — until later in the year.*

Todd Berrier, then Kevin's crew chief, was one of DeLana's good friends. Their fathers had raced together. She and Todd had grown up at the track together; they were "race brats" with a common bond and a deep friendship.

DeLana would oftentimes stop at the RCR Racing team hauler to see Todd to chat. She'd also speak to Kevin, just to be pleasant, but he'd always act a bit reserved.

"I would say hello to everyone, including Kevin, and he would give me this head nod that drove me crazy. I was not real impressed at all, but I kept saying hello to be nice. He always seemed shy and a little cocky." DeLana recalled.

That was the extent of the relationship until December. Todd didn't have a date for the team Christmas Party so he decided to ask DeLana to be a stand-in. Normally, it wouldn't have been a problem. DeLana, however, had a friend in town that weekend and couldn't leave her alone while she went to the party. Todd suggested he get DeLana's friend a date so they could all go together. DeLana saw no harm with that until she found out the date was Kevin. DeLana immediately went to her friend's rescue, telling Todd, "She can't go with him because he's not nice." DeLana then calmed down, agreed with Todd the arrangement was acceptable for just one evening, so why not make the best of it?

The night of the party the two young women were running late. Kevin, being someone who was used to things moving right along, was left waiting. After he made a biting but humorous comment about their late arrival, DeLana, who loved good-natured satiric wit found her opinion of the "young gun" beginning to change. The two began to connect on a different level. "Kevin and I have this sense of sarcasm in us. I guess we had a sarcastic connection," said DeLana.

When the night was over, Kevin said he'd call her for a dinner date. DeLana was a bit skeptical, but Kevin did as he said and phoned her the next day. They've been together ever since.

(Left) A job well done! Kevin receives the best reward of all for wrapping up the 2001 NASCAR Busch Series championship! (Opposite page) DeLana, no stranger to NASCAR-sanctioned auto racing, is keeping close watch over her husband's career.

(Above) Contemporary racing wives like DeLana can play an integral role in what happens on race day. In her case, she is just about an unofficial member of the RCR Enterprises organization.

(Right) Harvick considered himself fortunate to have his wife stick with him and lend support all during a hectic 2001 combined NASCAR Busch-NASCAR Winston Cup Series season.

"We just hit it off for some reason," she said. "It all just kind of happened without us really knowing it."

Life was somewhat normal as they continued to date and take care of their own business ventures. But they'd always meet and talk over the day's events. One in particular had been rough for DeLana, who vented her frustrations to Kevin. He responded by announcing he was going to Wendy's for a "Frosty" and did she want one? She was not amused with his happy-

go-lucky attitude and was in no mood for a milkshake! He went anyway and returned with a big smile on his face. He proceeded to light candles and turn on romantic music. DeLana thought he was trying to soothe her nerves and make her forget an intense day. He, however, was not only about to turn her day around; he was about to change her life.

DeLana said yes when Kevin proposed, and the two were now suddenly planning a wedding. DeLana didn't want the typical "racer's wedding" in November or December. Instead, because Kevin's family lived in California near Nevada, they'd have a Las Vegas ceremony. The couple never dreamed, though, that their lives would be turned upside down by the time they reached the altar on

(Left) DeLana was caught unaware when Kevin "popped the question." She recovered quickly, though, and planned their wedding.

(Below) Stung by the loss of Dale Earnhardt, the GM Goodwrench team had its spirits lifted on several occasions in 2001. One high point was victory in the inaugural Tropicana 400 at Chicagoland Speedway in Joliet, Ill.

Feb. 28, 2001, two weeks after the running of the Daytona 500. Kevin and DeLana were excited about the season because of Kevin's NASCAR Busch Series ride with Richard Childress Racing. The plan called for Kevin to run the full NASCAR Busch Series schedule and perhaps seven NASCAR Winston Cup Series events to help him prepare to "move up" in 2002. Kevin finished second in the Saturday NASCAR Busch Series 300-mile race at Daytona and was a

bystander for the next day's 500. On the last lap, Childress' No. 1 driver, Dale Earnhardt, slammed the wall and was killed instantly. The tragedy made headlines worldwide and left the racing world in a state of shock. It was at this point where Kevin and DeLana's life would go into "mach speed."

At 25, Kevin had not only impressed car owner Richard Childress with his driving but also Earnhardt himself. Dale, in fact, joked with Richard about stealing him and putting him in one of his DEI, Inc. cars one day. Richard undoubtedly knew Kevin was up to the task of filling the gap left by Earnhardt's death.

Kevin was about to take the racing world by storm — but not until he first wedded DeLana. The two struggled with the idea of getting married so soon after Dale's death, and DeLana asked Childress whether or not they should postpone the ceremony. According to DeLana, he said, "If we ever needed something happy, it would be now," so the wedding would go as planned, but first not without something of a fiasco.

The NASCAR Winston Cup race scheduled the weekend before the March 4 UAW 400 at Las Vegas Motor Speedway was the Dura Lube 400 — Feb. 25 at Rockingham, N.C. The couple planned to return to Charlotte on Sunday after the North Carolina race and leave for Nevada on Monday. That was without a rainout, of course. As luck would have it, the race was postponed by rain Sunday and rescheduled for Monday. DeLana recalled being scared to death they would not catch their flight and get to Vegas on time. After a trip in the wrong helicopter to the wrong airport, and then another chopper ride to the correct airport, they made their flight. The wedding went as planned, and their honeymoon would be spent at the Vegas track.

DeLana was just barely getting into the role of a driver's wife when the most unbelievable thing happened at Atlanta Motor Speedway. Kevin had finished eighth in the Saturday NASCAR Busch Series event. The next day, DeLana was in the pits watching the Cracker Barrel 500 thinking, "Wow! Kevin is running well. He qualified well and he is driving well." She, however, never thought he might actually have a chance of winning. Six laps from the finish, she watched Kevin take the lead for the final time — and the unthinkable was about to happen. Kevin won his first NASCAR Winston Cup race in the car Dale Earnhardt had driven only a few weeks earlier. She couldn't believe it.

"I was on the pit box by myself. I felt like I had lived an entire lifetime in that race. I felt like I had currents running through me," she said. "The one thing I remember so clearly was Jada Nadeau came up to me and said if Jerry couldn't win, she was glad Kevin did. That meant so much to me."

Kevin and DeLana were quickly sucked into a whirlwind. The decision had been made that he would run every Busch and NASCAR Winston Cup race on the schedule and pursue the NASCAR Busch Series championship, as well as the Rookie of the Year award on the senior circuit. This was not an easy feat for anyone, especially a somewhat untested driver with a wife.

DeLana traveled to every race with her husband on both circuits. At times, they hopscotched across the country like a pair of foxes trying to outdistance a pack of hounds. "This was a decision we made together so we did the season together, too," she said. "If he was going to do it, so was I."

The media attention was a challenge for DeLana, even though her background was in public relations. One of the obvious pressures was the constant comparison of Kevin to Earnhardt. DeLana felt as if it was a double-edged sword. "On one hand I was flattered because I thought Dale was the greatest race car driver ever and always will be," she admitted. "On the other hand, it was frustrating because Kevin is a different person and deserves his success. He works hard and the team works hard. No one wanted to replace Dale."

DeLana had never considered herself a "fearful wife," one who obsessed over the dangers involved in the sport — even after Earnhardt's accident. "I've been around racing all my life so I'm not afraid of what can happen," she continued. "I'm very comfortable with what Kevin does for a living. There is a time and a place for everything and, again, we have no control over when it is your time."

The summer months were extremely exhausting for Kevin and DeLana. She was working hard to be a strong supportive wife through the chaotic year, but there were times when she wondered if she could stand the pace. "The hardest part," she said, "was we did not have any time away from racing or the obligations that go with it. It was worth it but was still tiring."

Kevin and DeLana went into Rockingham in late October with the weight of the NASCAR Busch Series championship on their shoulders. Wondering if her husband could finish well enough in the Sam's Club 200 to snare the title there or would he have to battle it out in the last race at Miami, was almost too much. DeLana didn't think she could stand the anticipation another week — but by day's end her worries were over. Kevin captured the championship with DeLana listening on the headset during the final laps to hear if the points played in their favor.

DeLana believes she learned a lot about life during the 2001 season and certainly feels it has changed for her in many ways. "I cannot even describe how my life changed that year," she said. "I gave up my career to be Kevin's wife and took over the licensing of his merchandise for him, which was quite different from what I had been doing. I was also learning how to be a wife on the road which has its own set of difficulties because of the travel involved."

DeLana looks forward to the day when she and Kevin can have a little more time to relax in one of their two homes in North Carolina and Florida. She adores their two cats and three dogs and the joy she gets from being with them. "Kevin and I love our animals. They are so great and are how we like to spend our time at home away from everything."

Another of DeLana's passions is her own racing. Perhaps it was the fact that she grew up as a race driver's daughter that made her a racer at heart. She's raced Late Models at Southern National Speedway in Kenly, N.C. and would love to compete again. She and Kevin bought a Legends Series car for her to race, with him as her crew chief.

DeLana also decided that she missed public relations work so she landed a job representing NASCAR Busch Series driver Randy LaJoie. But what of the demands of working for one driver and being another's wife? "This is all a test to see if it will work out," she said. "I hope it will because I love my work, and I'm a good friend of Randy and his entire family."

DeLana sees herself continuing to stay involved in the business end of the sport because that's what she enjoys. "I like to stay busy. I don't like to just sit around. I can see Kevin and I staying in racing for a long time. I think about a few championships for him and maybe my own public relations company. Who knows? We'll see."

KEVIN HARVICK

This native of Bakersfield, Calif., has crammed more success into a relatively brief career in motorsports than many drivers have achieved in a lifetime.

Upon successfully competing in several forms of NASCAR-sanctioned competition, Harvick entered the 2001 season in a RCR Enterprises NASCAR Busch Series Chevrolet with 41 races to his credit. Team owner Richard Childress planned on running Harvick for the championship, and also entering him in around five NASCAR Winston Cup Series events for a bit of experience at NASCAR's top level. That scenario suddenly changed on Feb. 18 when Childress' star driver — Dale Earnhardt — lost his life in a crash on the final lap of the Daytona 500.

After regrouping from the tragedy, Childress made a decision. Harvick would stay in the Busch car but would also fill the gap left by Earnhardt. It was a long, tough year for Harvick but he got through it by winning the NASCAR Busch Series championship — and taking the NASCAR Winston Cup Raybestos Rookie of the Year award, too.

Born on Dec. 8, 1975, Harvick began racing Go-Karts at age 5 and won seven national titles and a pair of "Grand National" championships. By the early 1990s, Harvick was in a stock car and in '93 won the Late Model championship at Mesa Marin Speedway in his hometown. Moving up, he ran the NASCAR Featherlite Southwest Tour in '95, won at Tucson, Ariz., and claimed top rookie honors for the year. His next step was the NASCAR Winston West Series (the cars are actually NASCAR Winston Cup Series "clones"), and he conquered that division in 1998 by winning the championship.

Harvick then spent the 1999 season on the NASCAR Craftman Truck Series circuit where he recorded 11 top-10 finishes and prepared himself for the NASCAR Busch Series in 2000. It was another stellar season, as Harvick entered 31 races, won three, recorded 16 top-10 finishes, finished third in points and took the Raybestos rookie title.

Harvick's 2001 season included five NASCAR Busch Series wins in 33 starts, four poles and just one DNF (did not finish). On the NASCAR Winston Cup side, he won twice (including Atlanta in just his third start), finished in the top 10 16 times and won over $4,300,000.

JINA JONES

*ina Cadena and Roy "Buckshot" Jones had
been aware of each other since they were
both 5 years old. He played Little League baseball,
she was a cheerleader, but it was years later before
their acquaintance with one another would be
any more than just casual.*

"I knew him when we were little but we were too young to really *know* someone. It wasn't until I was in high school that we spent any time around each other," recalled Jina. "We went to different elementary and high schools but we had a mutual friend. His best friend, Randy Span, was my best friend, Dena Span's brother. In high school I started hanging out with Buckshot's sister, Laytona. I thought Buckshot was real immature then so I really didn't like him that much. We would get together at different times over the years but just as friends. It wasn't until after we graduated from high school that I actually started to like him."

In 1988 Buckshot was a student at the University of Georgia, majoring in business, and Gina worked for an obstetrics/gynecology specialist in Atlanta. He was also racing stock cars by then and had a local following. Jina and some friends heard he was racing at Lanier (Ga.) Raceway, a short track north of Atlanta, and decided to go. Afterward, she rode with Buckshot back to Dena's place and "we ended up talking until six in the morning. I felt different about him after that night. We got together again at Dena's for a party on another night. That is when we knew that we liked each other as more than just friends."

Being friends for most of their lives, things heated up in somewhat of an awkward way. "It was a little weird at first," Gina admitted. "Before that, we would talk every few months as friends, so things really changed for us after that party. He asked me out on a date and that was different, too. I had no idea how I really felt about it but I knew I liked him."

Jina and Buckshot continued to go with each other for three years until they decided it was best to break up. Their lives seemed to be diverging and both were dating other people. It would be three years before they'd get back together again. In the interim Buckshot was still competing at Lanier, and Jina had gone back to school to be an ultrasound technician. "We started talking and began to be friends again." They got back together when romantic relationships for both "fell apart at the same time." They dated for four more years, and then Buckshot popped the question.

(Left) Jina and Buckshot had an on-and-off relationship for several years before becoming a couple. Then when the quiet and somewhat understated young man decided to propose marriage, he did it in a spectacular manner. (Opposite page) With Kolton Ray, the first grandbaby for Buckshot and Jina's parents.

(Right) Kolton Ray picked a good time to come into the world — between Thanksgiving and Christmas 2001!

(Below) Little Kolton Ray is welcomed to the family group. From left: Jina's sister, Missy Hall; her mom, Judy Hall; Buckshot's dad, Billy; his wife, Mary Lou; Buckshot's sister, Laytona, and Jon Hall.

His proposal was anything but ordinary. Buckshot and country music artist Tracy Byrd had met at a race and became friends. They kept in touch, and when Tracy found out he was playing in the Atlanta area, he got Buckshot and Jina tickets to his show.

"Buckshot rented a limo for us to go with some friends to the concert. I was getting dressed in jeans and country concert attire. I was told I had to dress 'dressy,' which I thought was funny," she said. "I finally got ready and on the way to the concert, I realized I'd left the tickets at home. We had to go back, and when we finally got there, Tracy introduced Buckshot and

called him up on the stage with him. When Buckshot got up there he started talking about me and called me up there with him too. He got down on one knee and proposed right there in front of everyone. Of course, I said yes."

Jina, who wanted a large, traditional wedding, was overwhelmed with the logistics. She, however, got an unexpected early wedding gift to lighten her load. "I was trying to plan everything for our wedding and get it all worked out. Buckshot's dad called and said something like, 'What about December 19 with this kind of food, at this church and at this place for the reception?' He's such a nice man. He had it all worked out. It was wonderful."

The couple were married on Dec. 19, 1998 at the First Baptist Church in Duluth, Ga. Buckshot, who was living in South Carolina at the time to be close to his race team, moved his new bride to Spartanburg. "I loved it there. It was a nice town. The people were so nice to us," Gina said. "I was going to school during the week so I'd meet him at the track on the weekends. I liked to stay busy. I've worked since I was 15 so for awhile, I worked on Buckshot's souvenir trailer at the tracks to have something to do. I really enjoyed that, plus I liked meeting all of his fans."

Buckshot ran the NASCAR Busch Series for about six years before moving into to the Winston Cup Series full time in 2001. It was an unfortunate turn of events that would lead to a ride in NASCAR's top division. Buckshot and Adam Petty were friends in Busch racing when Adam lost his life in May 2000. Pattie Petty, Adam's mother, recalled a letter that Buckshot

Best friends: Dena Span and Jina. Dena's brother, Randy, was also Buckshot's best friend. It was an interesting connection.

Judy Hall was her daughter's maid of honor on her wedding day. Judy was also by Jina's side when Kolton Ray was born.

had written to her and her husband, Kyle. "Buckshot sent the most special letter to us about Adam and his friendship with him. It had nothing to do with him driving for us or anything of that sort. It just showed his sweet spirit and kind nature. His letter meant a lot to Kyle and me," related Pattie.

As Kyle and Richard Petty made plans for Petty Enterprises for the following year, fate seemed to drop things into place. Buckshot and his sponsor, Georgia Pacific, were looking for a car owner for the 2001 season. The Pettys were searching for money and a new driver, so all involved came to an agreement to "team up."

Jina quickly adjusted to racing on the circuit full time with her husband, but it was going to be different: She was expecting their first child. "We were so excited when I found out about me being pregnant," she said. "I had always been close to my family, so we decided to move back to Atlanta before the baby came. It was hard to leave Spartanburg, but I was glad to be moving back to be with my family."

BUCKSHOT JONES

Roy Jones was born in West Palm Beach, Fla., on July 23, 1970, but because his family relocated to Georgia so his dad, Billy, could build a cable television business, the Petty Enterprises driver calls Monticello his hometown.

How'd he get the descriptive moniker "Buckshot?" It has nothing to do with his love of guns — although he does like to hunt and fish in his spare time. Rather, after taking a spill as a child and then acting like nothing had happened, his grandfather said something like he was as "tough as buckshot."

Jones represents the latest generation of NASCAR drivers, as he attended the University of Georgia and graduated with a degree in business management. He started racing in 1991 at Lanier Raceway, a short track in Gainesville, Ga., and won his first Late Model race at Peach State Speedway in Jefferson.

Jones made his debut in the NASCAR Busch Series at the famed "Milwaukee Mile" at West Allis, Wis., in 1995 — he ran nine races that year — and returned to the track a year later for his first series victory. In 1997, he ran 30 races, finishing seventh in points, and the following year he competed 31 times, won at Loudon, N.H., ended the year with nine top-10 finishes and was voted the series' Most Popular driver.

Through 2001, Jones has accumulated 145 Busch Series starts, 33 top-10 finishes, three poles and over $2 million in winnings.

Jones ran his first Winston Cup Series race in 1997, in a car owned by his dad, and in five more the next year. In '99, Buckshot Jones Racing planned on a full Winston Cup season but cut back to 10 races and returned to the Busch Series. Jones picked up substantial sponsorship from Georgia-Pacific, a paper goods manufacturer, in 2001 and he became a member of the Petty Enterprises stable of Winston Cup teams.

Jina returned to Atlanta before the race season was over so she could get settled in and prepare for a November delivery. "I moved in with my mom until we could find our own home. I'm real close to her. When I got married, she was my maid of honor. When I delivered Kolton, it was my mom I wanted in the delivery room with me."

Kolton Ray Jones was born Nov. 26, 2001, four days after Jina's due date. With a baby on board, traveling across the country following her husband's career, naturally complicated things a bit. Gina's mother quit her job to help tend to her new grandson. That in itself was a godsend.

"Kolton is the first grandchild on both sides, so I don't think we have to worry about having anything for him," Gina said. "Buckshot's parents couldn't be happier to have a grandbaby. I have a great relationship with them. His dad is someone that I really respect. My sister, Missy, is also a big help and is so good with Kolton. I'm so blessed to have such a great family."

Gina's love of motorsports started long before her marriage. "I've always loved racing. I used to go to the Pepsi 400 with my friends before I even thought about going as Buckshot's wife," she said. "I love the sport. I love the competition. Buckshot and I both are so competitive. It's funny sometimes because we are both so hardheaded. We butt heads from time to time. We both have a dry sense of humor, which can be interesting. I would love for Buckshot to be able to race for a long time because I know how much he loves it."

Jina admitted, though, that becoming a mother changed her perspective about her husband's involvement in the sport. While the idea of standing by as he participated in high-speed competition rarely phased her before, motherhood seems to have increased her awareness of potential danger. "Now that we have Kolton, I've noticed that I am much more fearful," she said. "But I'll support Buckshot as long as he wants to race. I would like to have more children and spend some time at the beach when he retires, whenever that is. You just never know with these guys."

DONNA LABONTE

*S*he knew it the very first time she saw him. *She was just 17 and was a clerk in a Thomasville, N.C., Revco pharmacy. He had a job on a NASCAR Winston Cup Series team right down the road from the store. "I will never forget the look on his face the first time I saw him. The counter where I worked faced the doors at the front of the store. When I heard the door open, I looked up and there he was. I guess it was love at first sight," Donna Slate recalled of her first encounter with Bobby Labonte.*

Donna was still in high school, and Bobby was working for Billy Hagan's Stratagraph Racing team where his older brother, Terry, was the driver. Bobby walked into the store that day and caught the eyes of the young clerk. The two traded smiles, spoke briefly and then Bobby went back to the race shop to tell all the guys about the girl he had just met. Kim Labonte, Terry's wife, remembered that day well. "Bobby told me that he had just met the most beautiful girl he had ever seen," she said.

Both Donna and Bobby were very shy, so it took some time before Bobby got up the nerve to ask her out. He, however, was so bashful he couldn't do it face to face.

Bobby began frequenting the Revco as he found himself wanting to see Donna more often. This particular Monday night Bobby came in the store and talked to Donna for awhile and abruptly left right before the store closed. When Donna got to her car, she found a note from Bobby on it with his phone number. After a quick call on her part, the two were on their first date at the Pizza Inn. Only 24 hours had passed between her getting the note and that first bite of pizza. Donna and Bobby started seeing each other as often as they could during that time, although both felt that they were more friends than anything. Bobby was traveling with Terry on the race circuit and was out of town almost every weekend. Donna continued on in school and was preparing to go to college after graduating in May.

Donna received her high school diploma in 1984 and started attending nearby Guilford Technical Community College in hopes of becoming a medical assistant one day. Throughout her time in school, she and Bobby decided to leave their relationship "open." That meant if either wanted to see someone else they could but only after telling each other first. During this time they both occasionally dated other people, but no one could change the feelings they had for each other. Their arrangement continued for several years before things started to get more serious.

Donna graduated from college in 1986 and went to work for a neurosurgeon while Bobby was now starting to race. Donna knew it

(Left) Victory lane at the Brickyard in 2000. Years of hard work paid off for Bobby and Donna when everything clicked and the victory at Indy helped propel him toward the championship. (Opposite page) Donna knew very little about racing when she met her husband but today is one of the most "savvy" wives in the sport.

Robert Tyler came along in April 1994 and quickly became acclimated to the racing life. At age 8, he's already been in a Quarter Midget.

was getting to the point where she and Bobby needed to decide if they were going to settle down together or move on. They had been a couple for a long time — certainly long enough to know if it was true love or not. "I just knew it was time to decide whether or not to commit to each other," she said. "We had been together so long and we needed to do something." The two did start talking about getting married shortly after Bobby began racing full time in the NASCAR Busch Series in 1990. She had been working for the neurosurgeon for three years at this point. Bobby had just bought a condo and was seriously considering settling down with his longtime girlfriend.

Finally after eight years of dating Bobby and Donna got engaged in October 1990. Their wedding day was set for what the couple thought would be an off weekend on the NASCAR Busch Series tour, Easter 1991. When the '91 schedule was published, though, they discovered that the series was scheduled to race at Hickory (N.C.) Speedway on the Easter weekend, which was not a normal occurence. As luck would have it, however, both the wedding and the race went off without a glitch. The only catch was the newlyweds spent their "honeymoon" weekend at the Hickory short track. It most certainly wasn't how Donna had envisioned her wedding night, but she was with the man she loved. So as far as she was concerned it didn't matter where she was at the moment — as long as it was with Bobby!

Donna did not grow up around motorsports, so she knew very little about the profession that was also her husband's passion. She quickly came to share his ardor for the racing life, though, and traveled with him as he made his way through the ranks and established himself as a winner. Bobby formed his own NASCAR Busch Series team in the late 1980s and was always his own boss. He won the series championship in 1991 but really achieved his goals by advancing to the NASCAR Winston Cup Series in 1993. He joined Bill Davis Racing and after two winless seasons accepted an offer to drive for Joe Gibbs Racing. Success came, but Bobby and Donna found life in NASCAR's top division to be quite different from that in NASCAR Busch

(Left) The Labonte family welcomed another member in January 1998, and by 2000, Madison Elizabeth (with Mom) was enjoying her father's success.

(Below) Bobby has matured over the years and the once shy and introverted race driver shares his life with Donna, who has adjusted well to fame and success.

racing Series. "The pressure was much more for the drivers and teams than it was when Bobby drove the NASCAR Busch Series," said Donna. "I didn't really relax until Bobby signed with Joe Gibbs." Donna befriended many women as she was settling into her life as a NASCAR Winston Cup driver's wife. One in particular was Linda Rudd, the spouse of Ricky Rudd.

(Above) Donna no longer attends every race on the NASCAR Winston Cup tour, but finds life more "interesting" that way. She, of course, still fully supports her husband's career choice.

(Right) The racing life is hectic, and the Labontes make time for their children whenever they can. Sometimes a few minutes prior to a race means a lot.

Neither had children at the time and found they were quite alike in several ways. "I enjoyed having someone to talk with who could understand what I was feeling," said Donna of a common bond.

Bobby was becoming comfortable with his status on the circuit, so he and Donna decided to start a family. Donna had always wanted children of her own and this seemed to be the perfect time. Their first child, Robert Tyler, was born in April 1994. Their daughter, Madison Elizabeth, came along four years later. Motherhood on the road can certainly change things for a driver's wife and Donna was no exception. The days of "going light" were no more as she now had two children to pack for, along with herself and her spouse. "I did have a time there after Tyler was born that I had to adjust to traveling with a child and again when Madison came along," she said.

She discovered, though, a few of the "perks" of being the wife of a top NASCAR Winston Cup driver that made life on the road a little less stressful. For instance, she and Bobby now flew to each race in their own airplane and stayed in a luxury motorcoach while at the track. Donna fully understands and appreciates that life is easier for contemporary drivers' wives than it was for their counterparts of 20 — or even 15 — years ago. "It makes it so easy to travel with the children now. I don't know how the women used to do it before the coaches,"

she said. Still, Donna doesn't attempt going to every race on the tour. It's important to her that her children spend time home away from the race track, and "it's become more interesting for us when I don't go every weekend. Bobby understands that and is OK with it which is nice."

Donna doesn't consider herself a "fearful" wife, "I just accept what Bobby does which means I accept the risks involved," she said. "I've been around racing for so long now that I just don't worry. Bobby hasn't been in a lot of bad wrecks, either, and I do think that the more accidents your husband is in the scarier the next one gets. I will say I think I'm more aware of the risks now than before, but I also believe in the power of prayer, which is what calms me."

Tyler, just 8, is already expressing interest in the "family business" and has even run some Quarter Midget races. "It is different with Tyler than Bobby racing," Donna said. "Bobby is an adult and makes his own choices, but Tyler is too young yet. As a parent, you want to protect your children from things that can harm them so I do feel some fear with him — unlike what I feel with Bobby racing."

Though Donna would like Tyler to choose for himself a career that makes him happy, she realizes that racing is in his blood. His dad, uncle and cousin race, and his grandfather, Bob Labonte, began the family's involvement in racing years ago. "If it is something he really wants to do and wants to pursue it, then Bobby and I both will support him," she said. "If he wants to race, I will be there for him."

What does the future hold for Donna Labonte? "I don't know really because I am the kind of person that gives 100 percent of myself to whatever I am doing, which right now is being a wife and mom," she admitted. "I do look forward to one day being able to not go as much as we do now. I love to swim and exercise and have a vegetable garden in the summer."

Donna once asked Bobby if after he retired did he ever dream of himself sitting on the front porch watching their grandchildren play while she made lunch. His response: "Naw!" Whether the front porch dream becomes a reality or not, Donna cannot see Bobby ever sitting still very long. "He always has to be doing something, so I guess he'll still be involved in racing somehow even after he retires," she said. "Maybe not as a car owner, but if Tyler does race, I guess we'll be doing what his parents always did, which was go to all Bobby and Terry's races, so we'd do the same with Tyler."

BOBBY LABONTE

Obviously, Bobby Labonte picked up his passion for motorsports from his dad, Bob, and older brother, Terry. He started racing Quarter Midgets in 1969 at age 5 and then Go-Karts nine years later.

Born in Corpus Christi, Texas, on May 8, 1964, Labonte, with his family, "emigrated" to North Carolina to follow his brother's exploits. He got a job at Hagan Racing, for whom his brother drove, and said his biggest break came in 1986 when he was fired after Terry left the operation. That propelled him to form his own short-track racing team. He won the Late Model Stock Car championship at Carraway Speedway, in Asheboro, N.C., in 1987.

Labonte's NASCAR Busch Series involvement began in 1990 when, driving for himself, he finished fourth in points. The next year he won twice and took the championship. He won three times in 1992 but was edged out for the title by Joe Nemechek, in the closest points race in the series' history. Through 1998, he won nine races.

Labonte got a taste of the NASCAR Winston Cup Series in 1991 when he entered his own car in two races and failed to finish both. In 1993, Bill Davis decided to convert his NASCAR Busch Series team into a NASCAR Winston Cup operation and chose Labonte to drive. The combination struggled for two years and went winless. In 1995, team owner Joe Gibbs asked Labonte to take the wheel of his Interstate Batteries Pontiacs.

The marriage was an almost immediate success. Labonte won his first NASCAR Winston Cup race — the Memorial Day Coca-Cola 600 at Charlotte — and followed it up with victories at Michigan Speedway in June and August. Between 1996-99, Labonte won nine races and kept improving his position in season-ending points. His team found the right combination in 2000, as he won four races, finished in the top five in 15 others and claimed his first NASCAR Winston Cup championship.

The feat was record setting in the fact that he became the first driver to claim titles in both the Busch and NASCAR Winston Cup Series — and he and Terry became the only set of brothers to claim the title in NASCAR's top division.

KIM LABONTE

*W*hile Donna and Bobby Labonte paired
up because of that mysterious thing
called "love at first sight," such was not the case
for the first "set" of Labontes to come into
NASCAR Winston Cup Series racing. Kim and
Terry Labonte's relationship would take time
and a little persuasion, on Kim's part, to
develop and blossom.

Kim Robertson was a high school student in Corpus Christi, Texas, looking for a part-time job after school. A friend hooked her up with a title-clerk position at Bobby Young Motors, a used car lot in the Gulf Coast city. Terry was racing Hobby Stocks at the time and also worked at the dealership, which sponsored his car. In return for his labor, Bobby would offset some of Terry's expenses. Kim was in a serious relationship at the time and wasn't interested in seeing anyone else. "I really thought I would marry the guy that I was dating because we had been together for several years," she said. "Terry and I would speak to each other, but he was real shy."

A year went by before Bobby Young's two employees would actually go on a date. It was Memorial Day weekend and Kim and some of her friends decided to go out that night. She asked Terry if he wanted to go, never thinking he would. Besides, she was still dating someone else and was just being nice. To her surprise, Terry accepted the invitation. So, her first "date" with the future superstar also included four girlfriends. They headed to a nightclub, and when they arrived realized Terry was not yet old enough to get in, Kim used her persuasive powers to get him through the door. After the evening ended, Terry asked Kim for another date. Something inside Kim made her say yes. Their second date was near Kim's birthday, and Terry took her to dinner and a drive-in movie. He gave her a bracelet as a birthday present that she still has today. Kim remembers that night being the time she knew Terry was forever in her heart. "I fell in love with him that night. I knew from then on that I loved him and wanted to be with him," she said.

Kim and Terry continued to date quite seriously as his racing career was beginning to blossom. He won Late Model track championships at two speedways in 1976 and '77 but his family-owned operation was running short of money. That's when one of the track promoters introduced the Labontes to Louisiana "oilman" Billy Hagan, who agreed to sponsor the team. Hagan had a NASCAR Winston Cup team, wanted it to grow, and approached Terry about relocating to North Carolina to be a part of it. Terry knew he had to

(Above) One of Kim's most cherished mementos is this photo, taken just prior to a race her son, Justin, ran at Talladega, Ala. (Opposite page) Enjoying the good times: Kim's learned in about 20 years as a racing wife to accept what life can deal out. The one thing in life that is important is keeping a positive attitude and believing in a higher power than yourself.

The Labontes' marriage is just as secure and strong today as it was when they wed in 1978. She said she loved him enough to follow him anywhere and that included moving away from her family in Texas to go to North Carolina.

gamble and make the move, as his career might depend upon it. Kim also knew he had to go but couldn't stand the thought of being apart from Terry. It got to be such an issue with her that she couldn't discuss it without becoming emotional. Fully aware of how she felt, Terry found himself feeling the same way.

It was December 23, 1977. The couple had been dating for four years, and Terry decided it was time to make the relationship permanent. Terry and Kim were having dinner when he asked her to be his wife. "He just looked at me and said he knew I was upset about him going to North Carolina but that he wanted me to go with him," she said. "Then he asked me to marry him and, of course, I said yes." Her entire family was in Texas and did not want her to move away but knew how much she wanted to go. "My family knew that I had to be with Terry. I loved him so much that I would go with him anywhere."

Terry and Kim married in May 1978 and moved to the Charlotte area. Terry was a team mechanic and was away most weekends. Kim was working at Duke Power and had other temporary jobs to help make ends meet. She stayed home as Terry traveled with the circuit, hoping for a break. It came faster than expected. Hagan needed a driver for the Southern 500 at Darlington, S.C., and told Terry it was time to get into the driver's seat for his first NASCAR Winston Cup race. Terry caught the eyes of many with a fourth-place finish at the famous speedway and from that point his career took off.

Women were not welcomed into the sport the late 1970s. Kim recalled going to Martinsville (Va.) Speedway with Terry one weekend and she received a credential for the infield. It read: "Driver's Wife — Not Good in Pits."

Terry and Kim decided to move to High Point, N.C., to be closer to Hagan's Stratagraph Racing shop. They also were anxious to start a family. Kim knew about the difficulties of raising kids with a husband who raced, but she and Terry were confident that the time was right. "Terry and I wanted children, and I knew at times it would be tough, but I also knew it was what we wanted," she said. Justin was born on Feb. 5, 1981 and Kristen arrived on June 8, 1983. When the kids were quite young, Kim traveled with Terry as often as possible. She also developed lasting relationships with Pattie Petty and Ann Schrader, like her, two young driver's wives on the racing circuit. They are friendships that are very special, even more so today because of the years spent together through good times and bad. "It's good to have friends that are always there when you need them. Even when you don't get to see them as much as you want, you still know where they are," said Kim.

Over the years, Terry had proven to be a consistent winner on the NASCAR Winston Cup circuit and won the NASCAR Winston Cup championship in 1984. It seems, though, every racer will experience a "dry spell." As Kim noted, Terry was no exception. "It's always hard when your husband goes through tough times, but I always tried to encourage Terry. The one thing I love about our sport is the fact that on Monday morning after a race, the slate is clean."

Family portrait: At the 1996 NASCAR Winston Cup Series Awards Ceremony, Kim and Terry shared the championship with children Kristen, then 13, and Justin, 15.

© 1996 George Tiedeman

After one such slump, Terry, in 1996, put himself in position to win the NASCAR Winston Cup championship for a second time. After a long year of hard battling and two wins, he notched the title for team owner Rick Hendrick. "It had been what seemed to be a dry spell for Terry, so it just was so special for him to win it that year," Kim noted. "That was one of my most special moments in his career."

Terry and Kim's son, Justin, had become old enough to develop a passion of his own for the sport. He was dead set on making it his career path just as his dad and Uncle Bobby had. Kim, who always worried about her husband's well-being in a race car, was now facing the same thing with her son. "I have always been very nervous when Terry was racing and now I was looking at my own child racing," she said. "It did — and still does — scare me."

Justin and one of his friends, Adam Petty, had a lot in common. Adam's father, Kyle, also raced. The two boys had grown up together at the track. They went to school together and worked together toward their dream of continuing the family tradition. Kim remembered Adam "from the time he was just a baby. He and Justin were both set on racing and made that very clear."

Adam and Justin were both just starting their careers when Adam crashed in May 2000 at New Hampshire International Speedway. Someone from the Motor Racing Outreach ministry called Kim and told her that Adam had been in a bad accident. Would she please go to the Petty home and stay with Pattie? Kim hurried to her longtime friend's side, never imagining the news she would get when she arrived. "I walked in the door and Pattie had just found out that Adam had died. It was the worst thing I have ever been through," Kim recalled. "My heart just broke for Pattie."

Through the years, Kim has been a steadfast friend to Pattie but still cannot imagine the heartache and pain she's gone through. "I still don't know what to say about losing Adam. I loved that little guy and I miss him ... so what must she be feeling? Adam's death changed everything for me ... my life will never be the same."

She realizes the ardor Justin has for the sport is deeply imbedded. "I've come to realize that I have to be supportive. I have seen him miserable from not racing," she noted. "What right do I have to keep him from his dream? Terry and Justin race because they have a passion for it. It's not about money or prestige. It's their passion, so I have to respect that." Yet, what possibly can sustain this woman year after year, not only as a racer's wife but also as one's mother? Her answer: "God and me; it's that simple." One of her favorite keepsakes is a photograph taken at Talladega (Ala.) Superspeedway before Justin started a race. She was praying with him by his car. Someone had shot the picture for her and forever captured a precious moment.

Kim's spirituality got her involved in a leadership program in High Point that's brought her much peace and happiness. Kim is a "Young Life Leader" in her community, which is an outreach ministry for high school kids. Kim and her daughter, Kristy, were at a car wash several years ago hosted by Young Life, and she took a brochure home. When the April 1999 shooting took place at Columbine High School in Littleton, Colo., Kim fell to her knees and prayed that God would use her to help in some way. The brochure came to mind. She accessed the Internet to find out more and the first picture she saw was of Joe Gibbs, a highly respected NASCAR Winston Cup team owner and a committed Christian. Kim volunteered her services and meets every week with the other leaders. "This is something very special to me. My family has grown from this experience. Terry will even go when he can," Kim said.

This newest involvement, along with Terry's busy racing schedule, has kept Kim from struggling with classic "empty nest" syndrome. Kristen is away at college, Justin has his own home and ... "It's quiet at times but I do get to see them a lot," she said. "I can now go with Terry anytime I want without making plans for the kids, which is kind of nice."

Kim and Terry now own a ranch in Texas where they love to spend time away from racing. She doesn't envision moving back to the "Lone Star State" when Terry retires because they'll want to be near their children in North Carolina. Kim cannot imagine Terry not working with Justin after retirement. So it appears she'll have more years in auto racing but in a different capacity — that of a driver's mother.

TERRY LABONTE

The year that Terry Labonte first showed up on the NASCAR Winston Cup circuit, 1978, there were just two other Texans listed in NASCAR's *Official Record Book and Press Guide*. Walter Ballard, a Houston native living in Charlotte ran one race that year (he turned his car over to someone else for the season) and A.J. Foyt, also from Houston was an Indy Car star who ran just two NASCAR Winston Cup races that season.

Labonte, born in Corpus Christi on Nov. 11, 1956, started racing Quarter Midgets when he was about 10. By the mid-'70s he was racing Late Models owned by his father, Bob, but after a pair of track championships, the family's racing budget was about busted. Enter Billy Hagan, a Louisiana oil-industry businessman, who made Labonte an offer he found hard to refuse. Hagan had a small NASCAR Winston Cup team he wanted to expand and offered Labonte a possible driving job if he'd relocate to North Carolina.

Labonte accepted and found himself lined up for five races in 1978. In his first time out, he finished fourth in the Labor Day Southern 500 at Darlington, S.C. His career got underway the next year and in 1980 he won his first race — the Southern 500!

Labonte went winless in 1982, won once in 1983 and in 1984, 24 top-10 finishes, including two wins, led him to the NASCAR Winston Cup championship. Labonte left Hagan at the end of 1986 to drive three seasons for Junior Johnson's team of Wilkes County, N.C. By this time he'd picked up the nickname, "Iceman," for his methodical style on the track and terse speaking style off it.

After four victories with Johnson, Labonte spent one winless season with Richard Jackson's team and three more — also winless — with his old boss, Hagan.

Labonte accepted an offer to drive Hendrick Motorsports' No. 5 Chevrolets in 1995 and he got back into the win column with three victories. He won just two events in '96 but 24-top 10 finishes propelled him to a second NASCAR Winston Cup championship. That year, he also broke Richard Petty's record of 513 consecutive starts with a 24th-place finish at Martinsville, Va., in April.

WANDA LUND

W *anda Justice was born in the rolling* *hills of western North Carolina, in 1948,* *in a little town in Haywood County just west of* *Asheville. Waynesville, population 6,000, had* *never seen the likes of a petite fireball like* *Wanda before. At the time, of course, no one* *knew it, but she would one day be a highly* *respected racer's wife.*

Wanda spent the early years of her life on her family's dairy farm in Crabtree, N.C., a town of 150 souls. From the outset, Wanda was something of a tomboy, and her mother, Evleen, was worried about Wanda not liking to wear dresses like the other girls. One night Evleen discussed her concern with Wanda's stepfather, Jack Russell. His response was, "Don't make her stop milking the cows. She's the best help I have. Maybe she will grow out of it."

"Grow out of it" she did, as she spent her youth like most other girls, hanging out with girlfriends, school and, of course, boys.

In the early 1960s Wanda left home and moved to Florence, S.C., where she waited tables at a Howard Johnson's restaurant. Stock car racing was hot in the area — the famed Darlington Raceway was just a few miles away — so Wanda became a big fan. She was convinced that she would one day marry a race driver, and her first encounter with one turned out to be Bobby Johns, a South Floridian, who ran on the NASCAR Winston Cup circuit and sat at her table in HoJo's. He told her who he was but she was far from overwhelmed. "I remember thinking, 'Yeah, I know who you are but I am not as impressed as I would be if you were Buck Baker,'" Wanda recalled with a chuckle. The rough-and-tumble Baker, a two-time Grand National champion, was her favorite driver. Unfortunately for Wanda, he was already married.

Wanda's roommate was dating a boy, who loved to go to the Thursday night dirt races at the nearby Columbia (S.C.) Speedway, and Wanda would often tag along with the couple. One night in 1968 was special because all the "NASCAR boys" were coming to town. Wanda was 20 at the time and had one goal in mind for the evening — meet Buck Baker.

After the race was over Wanda was introduced to a 6-foot-6, 285-pound racer named DeWayne "Tiny" Lund by her friend's boyfriend. He was buddies with the imposing product of Harlan, Iowa, who had settled in South Carolina. The first thing out of her mouth was, "I don't want to meet you I want to meet Buck Baker."

(Left) Tiny Lund was one of the most well-liked — and, said some, free-spirited — racers of his era, but was also a family man who doted on his wife and son. (Opposite page) When Wanda and Tiny first crossed paths, nothing much came of the encounter. Tiny, however, was persistent in his pursuit of his "ill-handling hillbilly."

(Right) A dashing couple: Tiny traded in his driving suit for something a bit more formal when he and Wanda were wed in July 1969.

(Below) OK, they weren't the Beatles, (left to right) Tiny, Wanda, and fellow drivers "Little" Bud Moore and Buddy Baker knew how to jam!

That same weekend Wanda and her friends took off for a trip to Rockingham, N.C., for a NASCAR Winston Cup race there on Sunday. The race was over and everybody was getting ready to leave when Wanda noticed a big driver coming over to talk to a friend in her group. She thought that was the biggest man she had ever seen. She also noticed one of his hands was bleeding. When the giant approached her she asked him if he drove race cars. "You sure have a short memory," he replied. "I just met you Thursday night in Columbia." He informed her that she had better remember his name because he was going to marry her. She let him know real fast that her parents would kill her if she brought some big race car driver home, especially one that drove for "Big" Bud Moore. Before they parted ways that night she asked him about his bloody hand. Wanda giggled when remembering his reply — "ill handling race car." He would later nickname Wanda the "ill-handling hillbilly," a tag that is still with her even today.

Wanda went back to her job and her usual routine. Little did she know her life would soon be changing and in a big way. Wanda and Tiny's next meeting would be a little more dramatic. She never thought this big racer who seemed to be popping up in her life would actually save it.

Miss Permatex (left) and Wanda helped Tiny celebrate winning what was the first NASCAR Sportsman race held at Talladega, Ala., in 1969. Today, the circuit's called the NASCAR Busch Series.

Wanda went to Lake Murray in Columbia for a party one weekend. She didn't know how to swim so she declined to go on a boat ride. One of her friends told her to get a ski belt, wear it real low in the water and no one would notice she couldn't swim. She thought this was a great idea and was splashing around in the water when she noticed that Tiny had just arrived at the party. He came down to the water and told her that she'd better be careful because the belt could split. She was embarrassed that she didn't know how to swim so she acted like it was no big deal. About that time, the belt split right in two and under she went. Tiny immediately jumped in after her and accomplished the rescue. After he got her to the shore, he said, "I told you that belt would break."

It was that day that Tiny asked Wanda for their first date. She agreed because, after all, he had saved her life. When, however, the time for the date came, Wanda decided she did not want to go and stood the big Iowan up. Like most race drivers, though, Tiny was very persistent and eventually won her over.

They continued to date, and one day Tiny called Wanda from Darlington Raceway and said he wanted to bring another driver over to her apartment for dinner. He never mentioned who it was. Wanda was not a very good cook and she was quite nervous about preparing meals for anybody other than Tiny. He arrived and said, "You go get Marty Robbins from the track and I'll cook dinner so you don't have to." Wanda headed to the speedway realizing that she had never met the famous country music artist — and part-time racer — and he, naturally, would have no idea who she was. She got to the track just as practice was ending and hollered out to Marty to hop in for a ride to her apartment. He was so taken back by her forwardness that he demanded to talk with Tiny on the telephone to make sure she was telling the truth. "He thought I was some crazy fan trying to pick him up, I guess. He had to call Tiny to make sure I wasn't pulling his leg," she said.

(Below) Wanda's remained active and interested in the sport over the years and has met her fair share of celebrities — including Colin Powell, now the Secretary of State of the United States.

(Opposite page, top) Wanda was on hand when Tiny won a special event at Marysville, Tenn., in the 1960s. At right is track promoter Don Naman, who would become the first president of the 2.66-mile track at Talladega, Ala.

(Opposite page, below) Chris was just a toddler here at another of Tiny's many races.

When they got to her home, Tiny already had dinner ready and Wanda just needed to set the table. She remembered that she didn't have any napkins or paper towels. She frantically mentioned it to Tiny, who asked her what she would do if no one were there. She ran into the bathroom, got a roll of toilet paper and put it in the middle of the table. Problem solved!

After Tiny and Wanda announced their engagement, Marty told Tiny that if he was "marrying that little girl with the toilet paper, then I approve." He sent them a case of bright orange bathroom tissue for a wedding gift!

Tiny and Wanda now realized that they really did need to spend the rest of their lives together. Wanda had thought that maybe the 18 years between them would make a difference but realized that age did not matter. They were too much in love to leave each other and were married on July 21, 1969.

Wanda quickly adjusted to her new racing lifestyle. Women were not allowed in the pits in those days so all the wives would hang out together by their cars in the infield. Her best friends were Eula Faye Marlin, who was Sterling Marlin's mother, and Judy Allison. Most of the drivers stayed in the same hotels, which made it convenient for the wives to shop or sightsee in different towns.

Wanda remembered lying on the beach with Eula Faye one weekend in Daytona Beach, Fla., while Sterling was running around with a group of racers' kids. It was well known by Wanda's friends that she couldn't swim and was quite fearful of the water. "Sterling would always swim around me and splash a lot. I can still hear Eula hollering at Sterling in that Southern accent of hers, 'Now Sterling, don't you drown Wanda! You know she can't swim!'"

Wanda loved children and wanted some of her own. She and Tiny got the best news when they found out they would be having a baby. She had always wanted to have a family, and after Chris was born in 1970, he frequented the tracks with his parents on a regular basis.

One of Wanda's most special memories was one Christmas when she and Tiny were low on funds and so they decided not to exchange gifts. Instead, Tiny borrowed a Santa Claus suit and became the jolly old elf. He and Wanda went around to houses where they knew families who were down on their luck and handed out candy canes. Wanda recalled the funniest thing was the suit was way too short. "His ankles were showing and he looked so funny in that suit, but it was the sweetest thing he was doing. That was a special time for us," she said.

Life was good for the happy couple. Wanda, however, found it quite hard to make every event with Tiny so she started skipping them from time to time. The particular race was the summer 500-miler at Talladega, Ala., which was originally set for Aug. 10, 1975 but had been rained out. It was rescheduled for Aug. 17, but Wanda didn't want to go, so she and Chris stayed home. Wanda remembered waking up that day thinking something bad was going to happen to someone close to her. She just didn't think it would be Tiny. She called a girlfriend, told her of her gut feeling, and they decided to go see a movie to take Wanda's mind off her unease. She dropped Chris off with "Mom" Lund and headed to the movie and lunch in the afternoon.

Tiny was set to run a No. 26 Dodge owned by A.J. King, which was not his regular ride. He thought it would be a good car to race that weekend — his first

time in a NASCAR Winston Cup Series car in about two years — and believed he had a decent shot at winning. The race had just gotten started when Tiny crashed on lap seven. He spun out trying to avoid another accident and was T-boned by rookie Terry Link. Tiny was pronounced dead on arrival at the hospital.

The phone started ringing around town as people tried to find Wanda. Her mother had already received word of Tiny's death. The police eventually put out an APB on Wanda so that they could find and inform her of the tragedy. Finally Wanda was tracked down at the fish camp (restaurant) Tiny owned in Cross, S.C., where she was told of the accident. She immediately called for her mother who was already on her way to be with her daughter in her darkest hour. Wanda Justice Lund had just experienced her worst nightmare, the loss of her beloved husband. What seemed to be an even harder task at that time was telling her 5-year-old son his daddy would not be coming home.

The death of racing great Tiny Lund shocked the NASCAR family. Bill France Sr., the sanctioning body's founder and first president, and Tiny were very close. Wanda said it was the only time she had ever seen "Big Bill" cry. The tragedy shook many people in racing, including car owner King, who never again returned to racing. Nor would Link, who slammed into Tiny and was knocked unconscious on that dark day in Talladega. The crew of the #55 team buried Tiny's car in the hills of Tennessee shortly after his death, engine and all.

Wanda survived her worst nightmare not without many trying times and heartaches. She credits her family and friends for her making it through the tough times. "I have a lot of memories in racing, a lot of heartache, but we all stuck together throughout everything. Those friendships are lasting ones that are still there today," she said.

Tiny was inducted in to the International Motorsports Hall Of Fame, in Talladega, in 1994. Sterling Marlin, the son of Wanda's deceased dear friend, had the honor of bestowing the prestigious honor on one of his heroes. Wanda accepted the induction on behalf of her late husband. It was a fitting tribute for such a racing legend.

Wanda still resides in Waynesville, a town she's called home for over 50 years. Her son, Chris, is 31 and lives in Atlanta.

TINY LUND

DeWayne Louis Lund was born on Nov. 14, 1929 in Harlan, Iowa, and moved to North Carolina in late 1955. Because of his physique (6-4-1/2 and 270 pounds) and his good humor, he ended up with the improbable but somehow fitting nickname, "Tiny."

Lund was a racer from almost the beginning of his life right up to its untimely end on Aug. 17, 1975 in a muticar pileup at Talladega, Ala. His friends called him "fun loving" while a fellow driver said he was "one of the very best on dirt."

Lund began racing motorcycles at age 15 at the fairgrounds track in Harlan and a year later drove in his first stock car race at the same track. Actually, following a bike race, he entered his father's 1936 Oldsmobile coupe in a Jalopy event — without his dad's permission — and crashed it.

After a four-year stint in the Air Force (1952-55), Lund entered his first NASCAR Winston Cup race in October 1955 at Lehi, Ark. He crashed hard, spent some time in the hospital but recovered and moved south later that year.

In 1956, Lund ran 21 NASCAR Winston Cup races for a car owner from Cincinnati and the following year he ran six races for Petty Enterprises and 26 more for a team out of Taylorsville, N.C. The '58 season saw him run for several teams and also, with a buddy, haul moonshine from South Carolina to Michigan and ferry taxicabs back on return trips to make money.

While Lund is noted for capturing NASCAR's Grand American Division championship in 1968-71 (41 wins in 109 races) and the '73 Grand National East title, he is most well known for taking the Wood Brothers No. 21 Ford to victory in the 1963 Daytona 500. The team's regular driver, Marvin Panch, had received severe injuries several days before the race when he crashed while testing a sports car. The car caught fire, Lund and five other men pulled him from the blaze, and in gratitude the Woods put Lund in the car for the 500.

Lund ran 293 NASCAR Winston Cup races, winning three, and was second in NASCAR Sportsman Division (Bush Series) points at the time of his death.

PAULA MARLIN

*P*aula Hood and Sterling Marlin both grew up in the Harpeth Community of Spring Hill, Tenn., a small town just north of Columbia in the central part of the state. The Hoods and Marlins knew each other well, and Sterling's grandmother even went to Paula's church. It, however, wasn't the family ties that brought these two together. Rather, it was a date — but not a date with each other.

"I was dating another boy at the time, who went to school with Sterling. We decided to all go out one night but Sterling didn't have a date so I set him up with my cousin," recalled Paula. "We went to the drive-in movies. Sterling and I kept making goo-goo eyes at each other, so I guess you can say the night didn't go too well for my date and my cousin. After that, I kept going to the football games to see Sterling but it wasn't until a church hayride that he said he would call me."

Sterling did phone as he said he would, but it wasn't Paula, then 16, who took the call and agreed to the date. As she explained it: "I had just had my wisdom teeth pulled and was kind of goofy in the head from the medicine they gave me. I was knocked out for a week. I had a girlfriend at the house to see me, who accepted the date with Sterling for me because I couldn't talk. It wasn't until they were taking me to the doctor and asked what I was wearing on my date that I knew anything of it. I asked them what I was wearing where, and they said I was going out with Sterling. That was the only time that I was ever ready on time for anything!"

Paula and Sterling immediately hit it off and became an item. Sterling's dad, Clifton "Coo Coo" Marlin, was a NASCAR Winston Cup Series team owner/driver, and Paula began going to some of the races with Eula Faye, Sterling's mom. It was during that time that Paula began understanding the important role a racer's wife played in his life. "Eula Faye would do it all. She didn't have it as easy, like we have it now," Paula said. "Those women then were tough. She would go to races and chase Sterling around just to be there with Coo Coo."

Paula graduated from Franklin High School in 1976 and went to a community college in Murfreesboro not too far from home or from Sterling. Even though Paula's intentions were good, she did not quite make it through college as her parents wanted. "Lets just say college was not for Paula," said Paula with a giggle about her academic experience. "I couldn't keep my mind on school. I just wanted to be with Sterling. I quit school to be with Sterling and to get married. My dad said I got the 'MRS' degree from school, meaning I went to college to get married."

(Left) The Marlins are still as much in love with one another as they were when they first met. (Opposite page) They've also stuck together through thick and thin and are now enjoying the fruits of Sterling's success in NASCAR Winston Cup Series racing.

(Above) Exchanging vows for life.

(Right, above) Paula and Sterling with her parents and brothers.

(Right, below) Her parents on the left and Sterling's on the right. The Hoods and Marlins were well acquainted with one another.

"Sterling and I had talked about marriage. He had already given me one of the little pre-engagement rings. Sterling came over on Christmas Day in 1977. He pulled my dad over to the side to ask for his blessing before he asked me. My daddy probably thought we were too young but we got engaged and got married in July 1978."

Sterling, who was already racing at the time of their marriage, found a little apartment in Spring Hill for himself and his new bride. They stayed there until the birth of their first child, Steadman, who came into the world on October 29, 1980. "We didn't have much then, but it was enough for us to be happy," Paula said. "I would go with Sterling as much as I could when he'd go racing; a lot of it was local so it was not too hard to do. I always wanted to be a mom so this was an exciting time for us. I would pack up and go as much as possible. We drove everywhere, though, because we couldn't afford to do anything else. When I got there I would stay in the car with Steadman. I would hang around with Eula Faye, Nancy Langley and Colleen Baker during those times. They were a hoot."

Sterling worked hard, both at the track and away from it, and finally put himself in a position to build a home on 500 acres in Spring Hill. "We knew we wanted to stay near home and not move away from our families especially since we started our own family. We bought the land in hopes of staying there forever," she said. "We still live there today." said Paula.

In 1988, Sterling and Paula went through a very difficult period as Sterling lost his mother, then 54, to breast cancer. Sterling was in the second season of what would turn out to be a four-year run with Billy Hagan's NASCAR Winston Cup team and still hadn't won a race. "This was such a hard time. She had suffered so much," Paula recalled. "It broke my heart to see her go through what she did. I hated it for Sterling and our whole family.

"It was hard to imagine at that time how it would be without her around, but we knew we had to go on."

Paula and Sterling welcomed their second child, Sutherlin, on March 5, 1990, about two years after Eula Faye passed away and almost 10 years after Steadman was born.

"Boy, things were so different from the time Steadman was a baby at the track to when Sutherlin was born but still not like it is now," she said. "I used to keep Sutherlin in the a playpen with other kids at the track to keep her occupied."

Even after the better part of 25 years around the sport, Paula frankly admitted to still being "full of fear when Sterling races." She vividly recalled her most frightening experience, April 14, 1991, when her husband, driving Junior Johnson's No. 22 Maxwell House Ford, crashed hard on the 17th lap of the Valleydale 500 at Bristol, Tenn.

"He hit the wall in turn one and I was in turn four. I saw the big puff of smoke but couldn't see how he was," she said. "I saw Junior running that way; I could hear nothing on the radio. His face was burned. He had third-degree burns on his legs. He hurt his shoulder and his elbow. We had to bring doctors to change the bandages for him at the track until he was

Victory lane at Daytona International Speedway was a crowded and happy place when Sterling won his first 500-mile race there in 1994. The scene was repeated again a year later.

(Below) Sterling, Sutherlin, Paula and Steadman have interests other than racing. For one, they're all huge University of Tennessee football fans!

(Opposite page) First taste of success: In 1980, Paula and Sterling enjoyed the awards he got for winning his first Winston Racing Series championship at Nashville, Tenn.

healed enough for us to do it. That is the hard part of this racing business that never gets any easier for me."

Fear being a constant reminder to Paula is now even more real because of Steadman's budding racing career. "It is funny about him racing because it wasn't until high school that he started working in the race shop ... then it was forget about anything else," Paula noted. "I remember when Steadman was about 6 years old we were driving Sterling to the airport. He asked, 'What do y'all want me to do when I grow up?' I said, 'Well, Steadman, you can do anything you want to do.' He said, 'I would like to be president but you have to read too much. I don't want to be a lawyer because they have to be too smart. I can't be a tennis pro, so I guess I'll just be a race car driver because you don't have to be too smart for that.'

"I laughed so hard. But I am seriously more fearful with Steadman racing than Sterling. But I know he is going to do it so I try to be there with him every chance I get. When I'm not, he stays with my brother, Jon, who is also his crew chief, so I know he is in good hands."

STERLING MARLIN

If any race driver exemplifies the old adage, "Never give up," it has to be Franklin, Tenn., native Sterling Marlin.

The only child of Clifton and the late Eula Faye Marlin was born on June 30, 1957 and grew up in Columbia. He inherited his taste for racing from his dad, who, better known as "Coo Coo," was a journey-man NASCAR Winston Cup race driver. The younger Marlin's introduction to NASCAR Winston Cup racing came on May 8, 1976 at the Fairgrounds Speedway at Nashville, Tenn., when he substituted for his dad, who sustained an injury and couldn't race. He started 30th and finished 29th, completing 55 of 420 laps.

Marlin, however, was no slouch on the 0.596-mile track, as he won division championships there in 1980, '81 and '82.

From 1978-82 Marlin ran nine NASCAR Winston Cup races for five different teams. In '83, he hooked up with Roger Hamby, an "independent" owner/driver, for whom he drove 30 races. He finished 19th in points and was named the Rookie of the Year.

Marlin bounced around with part-time deals between 1984-86 before finding a full-time slot with Hagan Racing in 1987. After four years without a victory, he moved to the Junior Johnson and Associates team in 1991, staying through '92. He finished second in five races but couldn't reach victory lane, so he landed a one-year deal with the Stavola Brothers for 1993. After just eight top-10 finishes he joined Morgan-McClure Racing and surprised race-watchers by winning the Daytona 500, his first victory in 279 starts.

In 1995, Marlin won his second race — the Daytona 500 — and backed that up with wins at Darlington, S.C., and Talladega, Ala. He won two more races for Morgan-McClure in 1996 but after a winless season in '97 he quit and signed on with car owner Felix Sabates.

A renaissance came for Marlin in 2001. Sabates sold the majority of the team to Chip Ganassi, who switched from GM to Dodge. Marlin won twice and finished third in points, tying his best effort. He got the 2002 season off to a fine start by winning two of the season's first five races and taking the lead in points.

When Sterling's not racing, the Marlins spend what time there is at home in Tennessee or at their lake house in North Carolina. And time is precious because of an annual schedule that includes 36 points races, two special events, test sessions and sponsor commitments. "With Sutherlin in school I am busy with all her stuff. I also like to cook which calms my nerves," Paula noted. "I do go to most of the races, even with Sutherlin in school, because she goes a lot, too, and if not she stays with family while I go."

While most racing families like the convenience of the motorhome life at the race track, Paula still enjoys staying in hotels. It's, she said, just one of her little idiosyncrasies. "I get too claustrophobic to stay in the coach all the time. I like to go to the hotel and go out to eat. We stay in the coach during the day at the track but not at night. I guess that seems weird to some people, but I kind of like things the way we did them way back when," she said.

Sterling is still "in charge of his game" as a race driver — at least as far as he and Paula are concerned — but they both realize the time will eventually come for him to hang up the helmet. Paula has already mapped out their future.

"I think Sterling will race another five years or so, maybe longer," she said. "After that, I would like to travel and take some vacations, which we never get to do. I want to go to St. Croix and places like that. I guess some of it depends on Steadman and his career path. We would still go to his races, so I don't know. It's hard to imagine doing something else. Racing is all we have done since I've been married to Sterling but I sure look forward to it whatever 'it' is."

ARLENE MARTIN

Arlene Martin, born Arlene Everett in August 1953 in Lake City, Fla., was a young divorced single mother with four kids living in Batesville, Ark. She cared nothing about sports and in particular auto racing. He was a young single race driver with motor oil and gasoline in his blood, who was living in Wisconsin and competing with the American Speed Association in the Midwest. A short involvement in the NASCAR Winston Cup Series had just ended on a sour note. He lived to race. How could two people with such divergent interests cross paths and later marry?

"It seems so odd doesn't it? It was 1983. I was divorced with four girls so I wasn't even interested in dating anyone at the time. I had really had it with men at that point in my life," Arlene admitted. "Mark's sister, Glenda, and I had a mutual acquaintance, so Glenda and I got to be friends. I really liked her a lot. She and our mutual friend kept trying to set me up with Mark. I was not at all going for that idea. He didn't live there in town. I had children. I was divorced, plus I'm about five and half years older than him. I kept saying no to the idea because I didn't want to have to tell Glenda that I didn't like her brother. They would not give up on the idea.

"Mark's father, Julian, lived in Batesville so he would come to town from time to time to see his family. Mark was coming in to town for the holidays, so his sister convinced me to at least give him a try. I finally said yes to dinner. I was really surprised that I did like him. He was not at all what I expected. He was humble and quiet. He stayed for a few weeks after that. He would call or come by to see me while he was there but we never went out on a date. We got to be good friends. We found that we really did have a lot in common."

Mark returned to Wisconsin a few weeks later and would occasionally call Arlene. He then began returning to Arkansas quite often. Arlene thought he was coming back because of his family but was surprised to discover it was to see her. They began dating in February 1984, both apparently realizing "we really liked each other more than just as friends. It somehow just felt right. Everything escalated pretty fast from that point on." Arlene and Mark split their time between Wisconsin and Arkansas as often as they could. Arlene was busy taking care of four children so things got a little crazy sometimes. "I would try to see Mark on the weekend the girls were with their dad so it didn't get into their time. It worked out pretty well for everyone involved."

The couple knew early on they had a relationship that was not going to falter. Prior to meeting Arlene, his one true "love" had always been auto racing. He'd been devoted to it since he started competing as a teenager and took little time out for other diversions

(Left) Arlene with Matthew, then age 3. At the time, she was still fairly new to NASCAR Winston Cup Series racing and had a young son to raise, too. (Opposite page) Halloween 1996 was spent at the race track.

(Above) Even before he could walk, Matt seemed to have inherited his dad's smile — a fact not lost on his mom!

(Right) Arlene and Mark's sister, Glenda, developed a lasting friendship over the years.

— including women. This, however, was serious. Mark obviously wanted to make it permanent and began discussing matrimony. The question, though, was when to set the date.

"We talked about getting married but in the far off future," Arlene said. "Mark mentioned that we should get married in midsummer, then he said what about spring? He came back a month later and said what about Christmas, and then it was Thanksgiving. He kept moving the date up on me. Finally in August of 1984 he said, 'Let's get married next month.' So we did. We got married in Memphis, Tenn., at the Peabody Hotel on October 27. We had a small family wedding that was beautiful. It was real nice. Amy was 11. The twins, Heather and Rachel, were 9 and Stacey was 6."

Mark and his new family relocated from Arkansas to Charlotte, N.C., after the wedding. They only stayed there two and half months before they moved again to Milwaukee, as he was still competing in the Midwest. They lived in Milwaukee for the 1985 and 1986 race seasons before coming back south, to Greensboro, N.C., so Mark could more easily compete in the NASCAR Busch Series. "Mark and the girls and I were living in an apartment. The girls were all in school, so I stayed home a lot to be with them," she recalled. "When I did go with Mark, the girls and I would stay at the hotel until the race started. We

would watch the race from the car because there was nowhere else to go."

Life for the Martins changed all for the good in late 1987 when businessman, engineer and racing entrepreneur Jack Roush came into their lives. Roush, who was starting his own NASCAR Winston Cup team from scratch, convinced Martin to be his driver. Mark returned to the series in 1988 and has been one of its leading drivers ever since. As Mark's racing career was now apparently in full swing, he and Arlene decided to have a child of their own. "Mark and I had talked about having a baby. It was hard to believe sometimes with all the girls running around," Arlene said. "We finally got pregnant and had Matt (Matthew Clyde) on December 17, 1991."

Friendships in auto racing go deep, and a relationship that Arlene has treasured through her years in the sport was one she developed with Kim and Ernie Irvan, now retired as a driver. "Mark and I really enjoyed being with them," Arlene said. "They'd have their motorhome near

(Above) At their 15th wedding anniversary party in 1999. They got married in 1984 in Memphis, Tenn.

(Left) At home the same year. Considering her husband's occupation, Arlene has created a remarkably stable home life for her family.

Arlene has managed to share Mark's success in both NASCAR Busch Series racing (above) and in the NASCAR Winston Cup Series (right). In October 1994 he won the Busch event at Rockingham, N.C., and followed it up with a NASCAR Winston Cup circuit victory at Atlanta the next month.

(Opposite page) The Martins celebrate another NASCAR Busch Series race win in 1996 at Darlington, S.C. Mark left the circuit for good a couple of years ago with a record 45 victories.

us after we all got them. Kim and I had a lot in common. It wasn't until Ernie had his bad accident (1994) and then his other accidents that ended his career, that I ever thought about the real dangers in racing. Because we were so close to them, their whole experience changed the way I looked at racing. We still miss seeing them."

In 1994 Mark and Arlene decided to move once more. This time, though, it would be permanent as they were settling in Daytona Beach, Fla. "Mark and I love it there. We used to spend all our time down there anyways," she said. "Matt was going to be starting school soon so we felt it was a good time to move. The girls were all getting settled in their own lives, except for Stacey who wanted to try to go to school in Daytona. She ended up not liking it and

went back to North Carolina to finish high school. We found this great lady to stay with her during the week while she was in school. It worked out fine."

Mark and Arlene received some devastating news in August 1998 when the plane Mark's father, Julian Martin, was piloting crashed, killing him and Mark's stepmother, Shelly, and stepsister, Sara. The event was highly traumatic, and Mark took the tragedy quite hard. He continued to race because he knew his father wouldn't want him to quit.

Arlene has never claimed to share the same passion for the sport that Mark has and attends perhaps 80 percent of the events on the NASCAR Winston Cup calendar per season. "I have to stay home sometimes because of Matt's school. He can't miss school now that he is older," Arlene said. "I appreciate Mark's love for racing, but it was never my world. I didn't come into it until I was 32 years old. I like it because it's what Mark does. I have never been overly impressed with sports of any kind."

Matt, however, has clearly shown that he does share his father's commitment to the sport. He has been tearing up Quarter Midget tracks in Florida making a name for himself at a young age. "Matt loves racing like his dad. I enjoy watching Matt and Mark do this together. Mark loves helping Matt with his car and his racing. I guess when Mark retires we will help Matt with whatever he wants to do with his racing.

"I keep thinking that one day Mark and I can relax a little bit. We both look forward to being able to slow down. I always said I wanted to be an archeologist; maybe I should do that. With Matt coming on in his racing, I know Mark will stay busy with that because he can't be still. I guess there is no hope for me," she said.

MARK MARTIN

It was probably because of Mark Martin's father, the late Julian Martin, that the native of Batesville, Ark., (born on Jan. 9, 1959) acquired a love for speed sport.

When he was 5, his dad would get the family car well past the posted speed limit and let him take the wheel. He drove a pickup truck when he was 11 and one of his dad's tractor-trailers when he was 12. All this set him up for a career in stock car racing and he began competing at an Arkansas dirt track at age 14.

After proving he could win — and knowing racing would consume his life — Martin graduated from high school in 1977 and got a second "diploma" that year when he captured top rookie honors with the American Speed Association (ASA), a Midwestern based Late Model touring series. He moved to Indiana the next year to work in the race chassis shops of Ray Dillon and became, at age 19, the youngest guy to win a national title — the ASA championship. It was the first of three straight ASA championships and four overall (he won again in 1986) and in 1981 moved south to open a NASCAR Winston Cup team run by his mother, Jackie.

Martin ran five races that year, a full season in 1982 and then ran out of sponsorship prospects and shuttered the operation. He raced nine times for three teams in 1983 and after seven more events with a fourth was fired and headed back to the ASA.

Martin returned south in 1987 to run the NASCAR Busch Series and won three times. He credits that success as a reason Jack Roush hired him to spearhead a new NASCAR Winston Cup team that would debut in 1988.

Martin had found a home in motorsports' top echelon and has been with Roush ever since. He won his first NASCAR Winston Cup race with Roush Racing in 1989 and through 2001 went to victory lane 32 times, finished second 42, third 51, fourth 32 and fifth 31. He's claimed 41 poles and over $29 million in earnings.

Martin was also a semiregular in the NASCAR Busch Series for much of his career and retired from the circuit in 2000 with a record 45 wins.

ANDREA NEMECHEK

ndrea Blackard was born in Myrtle Beach, S.C., and grew up there with her mother, Mary Meisenhelder. Her parents had divorced when she was quite young, and after she matriculated at the University of South Carolina in Columbia to study retail management, she was on her own. After graduation, she got a job in Orlando, Fla., and in November 1988 she met a handsome dark haired guy, Joe Nemechek.

Her father, Frank Blackard, was deeply involved in an upcoming charity event called the "Margarita Ball." Andrea attended it and was introduced to Joe. Mr.Blackard met the Nemecheks when he was an insurance salesman, had been friends with them for almost 30 years and had even vacationed with them. "So," said Andrea, "my dad had known Joe since he was little. He'd mentioned setting us up before, but it never worked out.

"I had just gotten out of a relationship when I met Joe, so I was really not looking for something serious. We ended up having a great time that night at the ball. We were all there 'till real late. When it was time to leave, Joe asked my dad if he had an extra bed in his hotel room. I think he thought I was staying in the hotel with everyone else but I wasn't. He called and asked to see me the next night. We went to dinner and got along great. I was surprised how much I liked him. He was so shy, and I wasn't so I guess I just talked his little head off."

Joe was living southwest of Orlando, in Lakeland, Fla., racing Late Models and working for his parents. He and Andrea began dating and took turns making the approximately 120-mile round trip commute between the cities. "I was still working so I had to work around my schedule, which was tough, sometimes. Joe moved to Salisbury, N.C., in 1990 to race which made it a little harder," she said.

In March 1990 Joe rather unexpectedly asked Andrea to be his wife. "He was living in North Carolina and had come to Florida to race at New Smyrna Beach. I guess he decided he wanted to get married. He asked me the next morning after he got there, and he didn't even have a ring. I think it must have been a spur-of-the-moment thing. I was sure glad he asked, though." Andrea followed her fiancé to North Carolina in 1991 and prepared to become his wife. They, however, still had many ties to Florida and were married on Nov. 21, 1992 in Lakeland. While Andrea "ended up being so sick" the night of the rehearsal, she was fully recovered by the time they said their vows, remembering the occasion as a "fun wedding."

(Left) Sealed with a kiss. Andrea and Joe exchanged wedding vows in Lakeland, Fla., in November 1992. (Opposite page) Several years later, Joe stopped racing long enough to pose, with Andrea, for this formal portrait.

The Nemecheks are avid lovers of the outdoors, no matter what the climate. (Right) In late December 2001, they enjoyed themselves skiing in Utah, while (below) the year before it was a fishing expedition in the Florida Keys.

Joe and Andrea settled into their home in Salisbury. Andrea went to work in Joe's race shop keeping books and running the office. "I had always worked so I was happy to have something to do that was involved in Joe's career," she said. "I continued to work in the office until I was pregnant with Blair (their second child) in 1999. I guess we realized we had someone else that could do a great job. I didn't need to be in there anymore."

Joe's career was in full swing, in 1997, when he and Andrea

experienced the best and the worst of what life had to offer. John Nemechek, Joe's younger brother, lost his life in a NASCAR Craftsman Truck Series race on March 16 at Homestead, Florida, four days after his 27th birthday. Andrea was pregnant with their first child. "John's death was terrible. It was a hard thing to see Joe go through and a hard thing for me to go through," said Andrea. "I have always prayed about the fear that I have for Joe racing. This made it a little harder for me after John died, but I knew in my heart that I could not ask Joe to give racing up. That would not be fair, either. You are always aware of the risks but you are

never prepared for something like this to happen. I learned a lot that year. The most important I think is to be grateful for everyday we have because you just never know what tomorrow holds."

Just a few months later, on June 11, Andrea gave birth to their first child, John Hunter, on June 11. It was a "blessing" that offset a low point in their lives, and Andrea was grateful that the "good Lord pulled us through."

Andrea credits her girlfriends for the comfort that she finds on any given race day. "Two who are especially important to her are Lynn Bodine and Catherine "KK" Craven, racing

(Above) The Nemecheks seem to have patented the "family smile!" From left: Joe Sr.; his wife, and Joe's mom, Martha; John Hunter; Joe and Andrea.

(Left) Enjoying the championship: Joe, in 1992, edged defending NASCAR Busch Series champ Bobby Labonte by just three points to take the title. Joe's younger brother, John, lost his life in a racing accident five years later at Homestead, Fla.

(Below) Best Buddies: Andrea has developed close relationships with several other racing wives, among them Lynn Bodine. Andrea relies heavily on her friends.

(Opposite page) Andrea and Joe have been through some rough times in racing but have been able to enjoy and appreciate the many good things the sport has brought them. What they cherish most, though, are their children, Blair Makenzie and John Hunter.

spouses, too, who are on the same wavelength. "I think it takes another driver's wife to really understand what we go through week in and week out with not only the danger and fear but the hectic traveling schedule with the kids and sponsor worries," she said. "It is fun to have them to hang out with at the different tracks, whether we are shopping or taking the kids to eat. I couldn't do what I do without my friends."

The Nemecheks returned to Florida in mid-November 1999 for a combined NASCAR Busch Series-NASCAR Winston Cup weekend at Homestead-Miami Speedway. Joe won the Hotwheels.com 300 NASCAR Busch Series event on Nov. 13 and finished 21st in the next day's Pennzoil 400. Following the race, the family boarded a private aircraft, flew to the Concord (N.C.) Regional Airport and Joe got behind the wheel of the car that would take them home. Minutes later, they were in a ditch. Joe wasn't aware that the road had been reconfigured and was caught off guard. Andrea, who was eight months pregnant at the time, was the most seriously injured.

"We were driving from the airport back home. It was Joe, John Hunter, Joe's mom and dad and me," recalled Andrea. "They had just put down a new road with no signs or warnings of

the danger ahead. We flipped a couple of times before we came to a stop. I had to be hospitalized for a week. I had a broken shoulder, broken ribs, a laceration on my face, a collapsed lung and a hurt knee. But thank God the baby was OK. Lord, we were so lucky." Andrea recovered just in time to give birth to baby No. 2. Their daughter, Blair MaKenzie, was born December 26, 1999. "It was such a blessing after the accident to have her born without any real difficulties or problems. Blair just brought a whole lot of sunshine into our lives."

With John Hunter approaching his fifth birthday, he's started to keep a watchful eye on his dad's career. While Andrea is naturally proud of her son, she's not all that enthusiastic about him possibly later adopting Joe's profession as his own.

"John Hunter loves racing and cars. He loves speed, so I'm in trouble," she said. "I do support that love and desire but hope and pray he finds something else he enjoys more. That's my wish, anyway. It's a weird thing about these kids. I guess you understand it because they're around racing all the time but they just really love this stuff so young. Same as their daddy, I guess.

"I love this sport, but I look forward to the day that Joe retires; I just get tired. I like to be at home. I like to walk. I love to snow-ski in Utah. I want to do so much besides racing and I want John Hunter and Blair to see more than just a race track. Maybe in the next five to 10 years Joe will retire and own his own Busch team. I do what I do for my husband's career, but I get tired of the hustle bustle all the time. Maybe one day I can watch John Hunter play baseball. I look forward to that."

JOE NEMECHEK

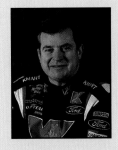

Born Sept. 26, 1963 in Naples, Fla., Joe Nemechek got his first tastes of motorized competition at age 13 in motocross racing. By the time he was 19, he'd collected more than 300 trophies and decided to trade two wheels for four.

He began competing at Lakeland (Fla.) Speedway in Mini-Stocks in late 1986 and in '87 claimed the Rookie of the Year title in his division. He joined the United Stock Car Racing Alliance in 1988 and after taking that championship switched to the All-Pro Late Model Challenge Series in '89. After being named both its top rookie and champion, Nemechek made the move to the NASCAR Busch Series in 1990.

That year, he beat out four other drivers for top rookie honors, and two years later, he won his first two series races and beat Bobby Labonte for the championship by just three points, by far the closest margin in the series' history. He also was voted the series' Most Popular Driver in '92 and '93, and through 2001, Nemechek corralled 11 victories, his most recent coming that November at Homestead-Miami Speedway.

Nemechek ran five NASCAR Winston Cup Series races in 1993 and went full time on the circuit the next year, running 29 races for Larry Hedrick Motorsports. He spent the next two seasons racing for his family-owned team, and from 1997-99 was behind the wheel of cars owned by Felix Sabates.

In September 1999, he scored his first career NASCAR Winston Cup victory at Loudon, N.H., but it was his only top-five finish of the year. He did, however, start on the pole in the second half of the year at Daytona Beach, Fla., Martinsville, Va., and Talladega, Ala.

Nemechek switched to Andy Petree Racing in 2000 and ended up with his best career points finish to date — 15th. The year included three top-five finishes and six more in the top 10. In 2001, he won his second series race, the Pop Secret 400 at Rockingham, N.C., but left the team at the end of the year to drive for Haas-Carter Motorsports in 2002.

LYNDA PETTY

*R*ichard Petty is one of the most recogniz-
able figures in motorsports. Indeed, many
people who are absolutely unfamiliar with racing
know exactly who he is. While his last season as a
driver on the NASCAR Winston Cup circuit was
1992, the seven-time champion is still revered by
many and respected by all.

The old saying, behind every successful man is a woman, is certainly the case with "King Richard." He and his wife, the former
Lynda Owens, first crossed paths 43 years ago and have been
together ever since.

Richard and Lynda met in their hometown of Randleman, N.C.,
when she was only 14. Richard, who was 19, was not racing at the
time but spent a lot of time traveling with his father, legendary racer
Lee Petty — one of NASCAR's first drivers. Lynda was starting high
school, as Richard was finishing up. She found herself around
Richard all the time because one of her friends was dating Richard's
brother, Maurice. As Lynda recalls it, the relationship "was more on a
friendly basis at first. We were just kind of hanging out, I guess you
could say, nothing big," she said.

Richard completed school and kept traveling with his dad while
Lynda continued on with her studies. Their acquaintanceship turned
from being friends to much more as time went on. "I think it just
kind of happened without us really realizing it. It was just one of
those unexplained things," said Lynda of the blossoming attraction.

In July 1958, Richard, 21, started what would become a long and
successful racing career that would culminate with winning a record
200 NASCAR Winston Cup races and a record-tying seven national
championships. "It was obvious from the start that Richard was
totally dedicated to racing. Racing was, and still is, his life," said
Lynda, who admitted that she wondered if he would ever want to
settle down. "He liked being with me, but he sure liked those cars —
plus he was traveling a lot at the time — so it was hard to get to see
him as much as I wanted to."

This friendly, candid woman didn't have to wait too long to find
out where life was taking her. In the summer of 1959, out of the blue
Richard said, "Lets get married." It did not take any convincing on
Lynda's part. They eloped to Chesterfield, S.C., just a few miles down
the road from Randleman. They were truly ecstatic about their marriage. They just hoped everyone else in their families would feel the
same way because they "conveniently" did not tell anyone of their
plans. Lynda recalls this of the wedding day: "We got married and

*(Left) Lynda Petty has probably seen more changes in the NASCAR
Winston Cup Series — and the position of women in it — than any wife
on the circuit. (Opposite page) Lynda and Richard are considered by
many to be the sport's "first couple." They've worked together to help
make racing as popular as the so-called "stick-and-ball" pastimes.*

had to come home and break the news to everyone. Luckily, our families came around and celebrated the news but only after a bit of convincing."

Lynda was thrilled to become Richard's spouse. Her ambition in life was "to be a wife and mother." She could not wait to have children so they started their family right away. Kyle, the first of four children for Richard and Lynda, was born on June 2, 1960. Lynda had her children like stair steps. Daughters Sharon, Lisa and Rebecca were all born over the course of the next few years, right behind big brother, Kyle.

Richard was racing full time and traveling several nights a week at this point in their lives. Racing had become a bigger sport and was keeping Richard on the road more than Lynda wanted at times, but she understood the passion that he had for racing and was not about to ask him to not follow his dream. She also was as busy at home taking care of their brood. Lynda would go to the races with Richard as often as she could, and this would include taking the kids along.

Once Lynda and Richard decided to wed, they eloped to South Carolina without first telling their families. It ruffled some feathers, but everyone soon accepted the marriage.

"It was always a job to get us all there," she recalled. "One year I got a station wagon and drove it to the track. I thought I had died and gone to heaven. It was our life, though, so we made the best out of it. Besides that, I had made friends with other drivers' wives and we would all watch the races together." Some of those special friends all those years ago were Colleen Baker, who was married to fellow racer Buddy Baker and Nancy Langley, the wife of Elmo Langley, an "independent" driver/team owner. "We used to have the best time together. We would laugh until our sides hurt," said Lynda about her girlfriends.

Though Linda had her share of fun in her early years as a racer's wife, she also went through a few heart-wrenching times. One in particular occurred on May 2, 1975 during the Winston 500 at Talladega, Ala. Lynda's 20-year-old brother, Randy Owens, was a Petty Enterprises crewman working in the pits during the race. On the 141st lap, a wheel bearing on the No. 43 Dodge caught fire, and Richard pulled onto pit road. Randy grabbed a pressurized water tank and headed toward the blaze. The tank exploded, and Randy died from the injuries he sustained during the freak accident. Lynda remembers the tragedy as if it were yesterday. "That was the worst thing to have ever happened to my family. He was the only boy in my family. My daddy never got over his death." What broke Lynda's heart even more was the fact that he was married and had two little boys who would now grow up without their dad. "I hated it for Travis and Trent because they were so young and it was such a horrible thing to lose their father."

When asked about her fear for her husband's well being in racing's formative years when the safety equipment available to drivers on today's NASCAR Winston Cup circuit wasn't available, she admitted that fear had always been a part of racing for her, but she tried not to think about it all the time. "You just had to learn to brace yourself to what could happen. That sounds terrible but I think it is the truth. I just never let my guard down," she said.

Richard and Lynda always stressed to their four children that they could do anything they wanted if they just put their minds to it. While their three daughters were doing the normal "girl things" growing up, Kyle was plotting his own path into racing. So now Lynda, the wife of a racer, was about to become the mother of one, too! This, however, was no big surprise. "When racing is all Kyle knew and all he has been around, I just don't guess you can expect him to want to do anything else," she said.

It would not be long before Kyle would get married and start a life of his own that would someday include grandchildren, or so Lynda hoped. The girls were also of the age where Lynda had a little more flexibility to travel with Richard. She, however, could not help but anticipate the day when she and Richard could do some traveling and go somewhere besides a race track. "I remember looking forward to the day that Richard and I could travel together and do some other things other than racing." It was also during that time that she began accumulating and displaying dolls in their home. "I just fell in love with dolls. I love to show them off because they are all so pretty. I have so many dolls; I can't even count them all. I think it is over 600," Lynda said. Even today the collection is on exhibit at the Petty homestead.

Racing continued to grow and change, as did the demands on the drivers and teams. By the mid-1980s, Kyle had become an established racer on the NASCAR Winston Cup circuit and a few seasons later Richard began to contemplate winding down his long career. He and Lynda talked at length about his retirement as a driver, and after many conversations they

(Left) Lynda kept up with her husband's constantly being at the track through his final season as a driver. She's since cut her travel schedule quite a bit.

(Below) Even other racing "celebrities" seek out the Pettys. They were happy to pose here with Herb Thomas, who won the NASCAR Winston Cup championship in 1951 and '53.

(Below) Lynda's travels have included more than just going to race tracks. She enjoyed a trip to Australia in the 1980s when several NASCAR Winston Cup drivers ran a special event on a super-speedway near Melbourne.

(Bottom) Travels aside, Lynda and Richard have never strayed far from Level Cross/Randleman, N.C., and have a comfort-able "spread" near the racing compound.

decided that "The King" would call it quits at the end of the '92 season. "This was a hard decision to make but it was the right one. We were tired and it was time for Richard to focus on being a car owner and not a driver anymore," she said.

The 1992 "Fan Appreciation Tour" was long and grueling but one they felt was necessary, especially for all the many loyal Petty fans. It actually began before February Speedweeks in Daytona with numerous radio and TV interviews, stories in the print media and testimonial dinners and ended Nov. 15 at Atlanta Motor Speedway. Richard was involved in a crash early in the Hooters 500 and his Pontiac caught fire. He got the car back to the garage, repairs were made and NASCAR's all-time winner returned late in the event to salute his fans and take a final checkered flag. Linda was exhausted when it was over, noting, "We knew it would be hard, but it was important to us to have it that way."

Richard and Lynda moved on to a different phase of their lives. They were now the proud grandparents of eleven grandchildren and Richard was in his "retirement" years. Well, sort of. "What retirement?" asked Lynda. She felt that the pressure associated with the team's spotty performance had made things more stressful than ever. For her husband, things had become no easier as "just" a car owner. She said his so-called retirement was not really like retiring at all. "He was still there at the track almost every week-end," she said. "The only difference was I didn't go every weekend like I used to. I wanted to garden and be at home with the grandkids." She still looks forward to the day that Richard might not feel the need to be at every race so that they can finally travel and do other things that she has always wanted to do with her husband.

Richard was running Petty Enterprises. Kyle was racing full time on the NASCAR Winston Cup cir-cuit and, lo and behold, along would come another racing Petty. Adam, the older son of Kyle and his wife, Pattie, now had his eye on his own racing career. That would mean that Lynda would now have a grandson racing. "I knew he would want to race because he was so determined. He was a deter-mined young man," Lynda said.

One of Lynda's most special family moments was when young Adam won an Automobile Racing Club of America (ARCA) race at Lowe's Motor Speedway in October 1998. With the victory, Adam, at 18 years and 3 months, became the youngest driver in ARCA history to win a super-speedway event. It was a bit ironic, as Adam had taken the record from his dad, who won an ARCA event at Daytona International Speedway in 1979 when he was 18 years and eight months old. "I can still remember how proud Richard and Kyle were of Adam that day. That overshadowed any of Richards wins," Lynda said. It was a special day for the entire Petty family — and their fans, too — because not only was Adam a fourth generation driver but he won in front of a "hometown" crowd.

That memory would later become one to cherish forever for Lynda as she would have to face the ultimate loss, the death of a grandchild not too long after that extraordinary day.

It was May 12, 2000 and Adam was at New Hampshire International Speedway in Loudon

RICHARD PETTY

Richard Lee Petty inherited a love of NASCAR Winston Cup racing from his late father, Lee, who founded Petty Enterprises in 1949, and took the company — and the entire sport — to a much higher level than it had ever been.

Petty, the older of two sons was born on July 2, 1937 in Randleman, N.C., which has always been his home. He grew up around the sport and was in the pits with his father at the first Winston Cup event on June 19, 1949 at a long-gone dirt track in Charlotte, N.C. Starting at the bottom — floor sweeper, runner and fledgling mechanic — Petty 's first time in a race car came on July 12, 1958 when he finished sixth in a 100-mile dirt race at Columbia (S.C.) Speedway. He also ran nine NASCAR Winston Cup races that year and 22 more in 1959. He broke into the NASCAR Winston Cup win column for the first time on Feb. 28, 1960 on the Charlotte Fairgrounds half-mile dirt track. Twenty-one cars started and just seven finished. The 22-year-old captured two more victories and finished the year with 30 top-10 finishes in 40 starts.

From that point on, he's gone 17 more seasons winning at least two races a year. He went without a victory in 1978 and '82, won three times in 1983 with his final two trips to victory lane coming in 1984. He continued on as a driver until the end of the 1992 season, completing his career as a driver with a "Fan Appreciation Tour" and a record 200 NASCAR Winston Cup Series victories.

In between the first win and the last Petty assembled an almost untouchable resume. Included are a record-tying seven championships, seven victories in the Daytona 500, 27 wins in 1967 — including 10 in a row — and a total of 1,185 career starts.

Petty has won numerous awards and honors over the years, has lent his name to a variety of worthy causes and continues to help shepherd the company his father founded over 50 years ago.

entered in a NASCAR Busch Series race. He wrecked during a practice session and died instantly. The news of his passing was as traumatic for Lynda as losing her brother in 1975. A woman who had always been such a source of strength to her family would now meet her toughest challenge. "There are no words to describe how my heart felt," she said. "It was the most tragic thing to happen. I could not stand what had happened to Adam and to our family. We will never get over Adam's death."

What started as pain and grief has turned into a project that will keep Adam's memory alive for a long time. Kyle and Pattie had, for some time, been working on setting up a camp in North Carolina especially for children with life-threatening illnesses. It was a project that Adam had gotten interested in not long before his death. This camp would be modeled after Hollywood movie star Paul Newman's The Hole In The Wall Gang Camp in Connecticut and would be open to children ages 7-15 from the Carolinas and Virginia. Richard and Lynda donated 60 acres for the campsite, which is scheduled to open in 2004. "This camp is where my energy is now because the whole family believes in it and it's something we can all do together," said Lynda. The camp was named "The Victory Junction Gang Camp in honor of Adam Petty."

Lynda and Richard still live in the same house where they've been for many years and in the same town where they were born and grew up. "This town is all people we have known all our lives. We don't have to be anything special to them except ourselves. I don't ever want to be anywhere else," she said of Randleman.

Although a museum is presently part of the Petty Enterprises "compound," Lynda has hopes of building a larger structure one day to house all of Richards's things. "Nothing is different. I guess we just don't really like to change too many things," she said. "I guess it is the same with my house because it is just a hodge-podge of junk — but it is home."

Lynda still goes to the track when she feels like it but admitted that a lot of her time is spent at home where she loves to garden and be with the grandchildren. "Richard and I are at the point in our lives that Richard still wants to go to the races and I don't. I'm better off at home because at the track, I have too much time to think," she said with finality.

PATTIE PETTY

attie and Kyle Petty are in the middle of renovating their home where they've lived for the past eight years. Their plan was to live in the 1,800-square-foot dwelling while they built their dream home atop a hill on their property, but as Pattie put it, "Racing has not smiled on us for the past few years, so we keep putting it off until next year ... but it never seems to come." Kyle, a firm believer in paying "up front," would never consider borrowing money, so their master plan, for now, remains just a dream.

"I laugh about the mess we have had in our little home year after year. Last year at Christmas we had plastic blowing over us because we were adding on to our bedroom. We just built a closet for me so things are good," said Pattie about the never-ending construction.

It's the little things in life now that blow over Pattie like so much pollen in the wind. The reason is simple: Much bigger things have made an impact on her ... things that have changed her life, forever.

Pattie Huffman, the daughter of Ven Montgomery and Margaret Huffman of High Point, N.C., was teaching school in Lenoir, N.C., and working on her graduate degree when she first came in contact with the famous Petty family. Kyle was still in high school at the time and working for his dad, Richard, at the race track.

Pattie was a lover of horses. She'd heard of the Pettys and knew of their interest in equines as well. Linda and Richard Petty, Kyle's parents, actually bought some horses for their daughters from one of Pattie's neighbors. The funny thing was Pattie knew they were the wrong horses for the girls. "Those horses were a disaster. I felt so bad for them," she jokingly said. "They should have bought horses from me."

While attending graduate school at Appalacian State University, Pattie would do odd modeling jobs to make money. One of her friends told her about a position in NASCAR Winston Cup Series racing that would suit her well. Actually, it was with the R.J. Reynolds Tobacco Co., the series' main sponsor. As its representative at the track — "Miss Winston" — she could travel to races on weekends and still go to school during the week. Pattie thought it was a great idea. She was hired, not for the NASCAR Winston Cup Series, but, instead, for the company's involvement in Camel GTX road racing. She worked in the Camel program until she eventually was transferred to the stock car series where she encountered young Kyle Petty for the first time.

Their initial meeting came in 1976 at the Fairgrounds Speedway in Nashville, Tenn., and Kyle was limping around with a broken leg. She went over to introduce herself and told him that she knew about the horses the Pettys had purchased and informed him of her

(Left) Pattie actively followed son Adam's blossoming career. His loss, in 2000, was a devastating blow. (Opposite page) Racing has treated the Pettys very well over the last two decades, but they've also had more than their share of hard times. Their marriage has, however, stood every test.

concerns as far as their selection. Actually, she let him know without a doubt that they had ended up with the wrong horseflesh. Her beauty and her wit took him aback. They befriended one another and agreed to keep in touch.

Pattie and Kyle did remain in contact, as she checked on the Petty stable quite often. She eventually gave one of her ponies to Kyle's sister, Rebecca. Not only did they share a love of horses, they discovered they enjoyed one another's company. "I remembered just really enjoying being with him," she said. "I didn't like the dating scene and I didn't go out as a lot of my friends did. I liked how I felt with Kyle." Pattie was concerned about her changing feelings for him. She was several years older than Kyle and was concerned about what people would think of the age difference. So Pattie conveniently took a female friend with her whenever she went anywhere with Kyle.

Kyle and Pattie would get together every Tuesday night at a Bible study class. "Kyle and I would go to this chicken place and then go to Bible study. We were getting used to being together and I was not sure if that was good or not," she said.

In the spring of 1977 Kyle, still in high school at the time, told Pattie that he was in love with her and intended to marry her. Pattie, thinking that was not a good idea, told him that they shouldn't see each other anymore. Kyle took her words to heart and didn't come around for weeks. It was during this time that Pattie realized her true feelings for Kyle and that she really missed him. She found herself looking for him at the race track while in her Miss Winston role. When she did spot him it would be from a distance ... a little wave of the hand ... which really hurt Pattie. She wanted to be with him but was confused. He had done what she asked of him ... left her alone ... but was that how it should be? She didn't think so.

Finally Kyle called her and confessed his feelings. He'd missed her over the three weeks they were apart. "Kyle asked me if we could start over. I was so glad because we were so relaxed with each other and I really did miss him," she said. "He then asked me to have dinner with his parents. Now that was a little scary." After a pleasant meal with Richard and Lynda, Pattie's fears were put to rest. From then on she would be a part of the Petty family.

Kyle proposed to Pattie in July 1978. He had just graduated from high school and had discussed the idea with Pattie several times. Kyle and Pattie were taking care of her yearling that Kyle had given her. He asked her to go to get some feed, and there in the trough was her engagement ring. Not only did Pattie have a wedding to plan but she also had to tell her supervisors at Reynolds that she had not only broken the rules of not dating anyone at the track, but she was quitting her job to marry Kyle. When she told her friends at RJR, they said they'd "heard something about that" but nonetheless were happy for her.

Kyle and Pattie were married on February 4, 1979 at Kepleys Barn in High Point, N.C. They had a "good ol' country pig pickin'" wedding reception that "was the most fun. It was just how we wanted it."

Kyle's racing career began about a week later when he ran — and won — his very first race of any kind, a 200-mile ARCA event at Daytona Beach, Fla., during Speedweeks. By then Pattie

Competition runs in the Petty blood, but in the case of Pattie and Kyle's daughter, Montgomery Lee, it's one horsepower at a time! Like a true Petty, though, she captured championships.

was traveling with him every weekend to the races. "It was fun back then because everyone was in the same boat. No one had any money. Everybody was there trying to make races," said Pattie.

Kyle and Pattie were thrilled when they found out that they were about to become parents for the first time. Adam was born on July 10, 1980, Austin was next on March 24, 1982, and Montgomery Lee completed the brood on Dec. 17, 1985. Having children at the track certainly creates a different set of circumstanced for a racer's wife. "It was hard sometimes carting the kids everywhere. I was always a strict disciplinarian, so I think that helped me keep some kind of control on the road traveling with Kyle," Pattie said. But traveling with the kids was not Pattie's idea of fun so she remained at home with the kids most of the time as they were growing up. "They had their friends and all the stuff that goes with that so I stayed home. Kyle was OK with that so it worked for all of us." Pattie learned from her mother-in-law early on how to be a racer's wife and a mother at the same time. "Lynda was, and still is, such an example to other wives in the sport. She exemplifies what it means to be a supportive wife and a loving mom," said Pattie.

With Kyle well established in the sport Adam was showing some interest in his dad's business. "Adam knew from early on what he wanted to do," noted Pattie. "He was so determined about it that you just could not help but get caught up in his enthusiasm." But as Kyle and Pattie respected Adam's ambition, he certainly would not get it without earning it. "We have always made our kids work for what they want. We could have handed things to them but we didn't. So, when Adam worked for his dream we helped him as much as we could."

Adam graduated from high school in 1998 and was determined to follow in his father's footsteps by developing his own racing career. He found some success early and was just beginning his journey when he lost his life in a practice-session crash prior to a NASCAR Busch Series event at Loudon, N.H., in May 2000. Neither Kyle nor Pattie were there that day, which is something that has haunted Pattie. "It bothered me so much that I was not there but I do realize it would not have changed the outcome. Kyle and Montgomery Lee were at a horse show in England so it was especially hard on them having to come home to such sadness," she said. "It was so hard for all of us. We still want him and miss him and need him. We will never get over Adam's death, ever. We just learn to get through each day the best we can."

Kyle took a break from racing as he looked at the future of Petty Enterprises and pondered what direction the entire company would go. "We were so hurt and full of pain that it was hard to even focus on the everyday things much less on our race teams," Pattie admitted. Adam was looked upon as the "future" of Petty Enterprises and was scheduled to race the No. 45 Sprint-sponsored Chevrolet in the 2001 season. After much thought and many prayers, Kyle decided to complete the rest of the 2000 NASCAR Busch Series season in Adam's car. "Kyle knew in his heart what he wanted to do and that was to get in the car," Pattie said. "In a way, I think he felt he was carrying on not only for himself but for the team. It was such a hard time for the guys. They all loved Adam, too. We all just hung in there together. Kyle did what he felt was best and we all agreed with him. I don't know how Kyle did what all he did when I knew he was hurting so badly."

Racing would certainly never be the same for Kyle and Pattie or anyone else at Petty Enterprises. Pattie, who didn't go to every race in the past, doesn't miss one now unless there's a conflict involving Austin or Montgomery Lee. "Kyle needs me there. We do better when we are with each other. For the first time he really wants me to be there as much as he needs me there. It takes the pressure off both of us when we are together," she said.

When not at the track with Kyle, Pattie goes to horse shows with Montgomery Lee, who is an accomplished rider. "I get so much joy from 'Gummy's' riding. She is so good and much like Adam, she works really hard," a proud Pattie said. "She is very determined. Montgomery Lee won Congress twice, in 2000 and 2001, and in 2001 won the World Championships. It was such a happy time for Gummy and for us. To see her work so hard and then reach her goal gave me and Kyle such joy."

Pattie's busy these days with a new project, The Victory Junction Camp, now under construction, in Adam's memory, on 62 acres near Greensboro, N.C., set to open in 2004. With activities such as boating, fishing, crafts, sports and fine arts, the camp will be a place of refuge and hope for children 7-15 from North and South Carolina and Virginia, afflicted with illnesses that include asthma, diabetes, heart, kidney and liver disease and certain forms of cancer. It will be modeled after actor Paul Newman's Hole in The Wall Gang Camp in northeastern Connecticut, the Boggy Creek Gang Camp near Orlando, Fla., and other facilities in New York, California and overseas, and it will be a part of the "Newman family of camps."

"This was something that Kyle and I got involved with sometime back, and we were trying to get Adam involved as well," noted Pattie. "Adam had gotten very interested in the camp. At the time of his death he was going to purchase 12 acres that was attached to our land to donate for the future site of the camp. The week of his accident he was to sign the papers. But with his accident that did not happen. We lost the land but Lynda and Richard donated some of their own land for the camp.

"It was so weird how it all happened. The Lord works in mysterious ways. Richard and Lynda had not gotten involved before Adam's death and now they both are very involved and supportive. Richard is like Daniel Boone out on a tractor clearing land. It has been so good for all of us." (*Editor's Note: Support for The Victory Junction Camp comes from individual and corporate donations. For further information write: 311 Branson Mill Rd., Randleman, N.C. 27317 or call (336) 498-9055.*)

When Kyle's driving career starts to eventually taper off, he'll continue to run Petty Enterprises. Pattie anticipates the day that she can slow down a bit as well. "We've been in racing for so long that I sometimes just get tired," she said. "I look forward to the day when I can sit back and see everybody I love being happy. What a blessing that would be!"

KYLE PETTY

While several racing fathers thought the best way for their sons to break into NASCAR Winston Cup Series racing was to gain some experience on short tracks before attempting to run on the super-speedways, Richard Petty wasn't one of them.

Once his son, Kyle, decided to make the sport his career, Richard felt the best place for him to start was on a big track. Hence, Kyle Petty's first race was a 200-mile Automobile Racing Club of America contest in February 1979 at Daytona International Speedway. He won the race and was on the way to following in his dad's — and grandfather Lee Petty's — footsteps.

Born on June 2, 1960, the Randleman, N.C., native is now the chief operating officer of Petty Enterprises, the racing team Lee founded in 1949. Commencing with Richard's retirement as a driver at the end of 1992, Kyle gradually assumed more responsibility for its operation while continuing to race himself.

He ran five NASCAR Winston Cup races for Petty Enterprises in '79, 14 in 1980, the full season in '81, split his driving time between the Petty team and another operation in '82 and two more complete years before leaving the team to drive for the Wood Brothers from 1985-88. His first of eight career victories (through 2001) came at Richmond, Va., in February 1986. That made him the first third-generation NASCAR Winston Cup Series winner. He won the Coca-Cola 600 at Charlotte in '87, but after no victories in 1988 left the Woods to start an eight-year association with team owner Felix Sabates.

Petty won back-to-back early-season events at Rockingham, N.C., in 1990-91, and four more races for the team in '92, '93 and '95. He ran two seasons in equipment he himself owned and returned to the Petty fold for good in 1999.

Petty has struggled with the combined responsibilities of being a team owner and driver over the last couple of years but has still brought in over $13,300,000 in a rewarding career.

DORIS ROBERTS

*D*oris McConnell was always a big race fan even before she married one of the greatest drivers of all time. Her older brother, Felix, used to take her to the races when she was a teenager. On this particular day in 1950, she was at a Modified race in Charlotte in the south end of town when she met Glenn Roberts. Better known as "Fireball," he got his nickname from throwing a baseball at lightning speed as a teen. He played on a team out of Zellwood, Fla., before he got into racing. To this day, though, Doris never uses the moniker, still preferring to call him by his given name.

"I was at the races with my girlfriends. We all loved racing and race car drivers. I used to always say that I wanted to marry a driver. I told my girlfriends that one day I would find me one," she said. "I was standing near Glenn's tow car when he came back to get something out of it. He asked me who I was pulling for in the heat race. I told him whoever wins. He went out, won the heat race and then came back to me after it was over and said, 'What about that?' I told him anyone could get lucky.

"When we left the race that day my friend asked if I knew where Buddy Shuman's (a local racer) shop was. We drove by it with me knowing that Buddy was in Macon, Ga., so I knew no one would be there. As we drove by the shop, Glenn, who was housing his cars in Buddy's shop, yelled out to me. He was standing there with two other guys. He asked if we wanted to go to dinner that night. Six people went to dinner. We had a wonderful time. He was on his way to New Jersey, as he was going to run the northern tracks. Three weeks later he came back to North Carolina, and I saw him at a track in Midland."

Fireball was not only a stud on the track; he was off it, as well. He let Doris know he was playing the field, until she let him know he had the best thing in her. "I saw Glenn several times at different tracks, but then he started dating one of my friends. He finally asked me out after he figured out I was the one for him," she said laughing.

Their first evening out was the "typical racer's date" — spend it with your man in the race shop. "He called me to ask me out on a date and when he did he asked, 'Can you drive to Charlotte?' I sat in Buddy's shop and watched Glenn change out the engine. It wasn't very romantic, but it was Glenn. He did ask me to go with him the next day to a race in Hendersonville. We just kind of hit it off from there."

Doris, who had always wanted to marry a racer, was about to have her wish come true. "I was at the drive-in restaurant with Glenn when he said, 'I think it's time to get married.' I said, 'Are

(Left) Victory lane at Hillsboro, N.C., Aug. 13, 1950: Married for just three weeks, Doris and Fireball celebrated his first career NASCAR Winston Cup victory. (Opposite page) Today, as one of NASCAR's "first" ladies, Doris leads an active life and keeps her former husband's memory alive.

(Right) At Darlington (S.C.) Raceway in 1958, Fireball appeared to be relaxed before he won the Labor Day classic, the Southern 500.

(Below) Mr. And Mrs. Roberts, with the winner's hardware at Daytona Beach in Feb. 1962. That year, he made a clean sweep there by winning three events during Speedweeks and the 400-miler in July.

you asking me to marry you?' I, of course, said yes. I couldn't believe it, I had only known him a month."

Fireball and Doris married three weeks later on July 22, 1950 in York, S.C. "Eloping" to South Carolina for the nuptials wasn't Fireball's idea. When he told Bill France Sr., his plans, the NASCAR president suggested having the ceremony at the Charlotte Fairgrounds track on a Friday night. Doris, however, was adamantly opposed to the idea. She got her way, and they drove across the state line and found a justice of the peace. Also, Doris' parents, Ila and Felix McConnell Sr., were unsure of her marrying a man with such a dubious profession, but she assured them she was "doing the right thing." Doris and Fireball moved in with her family in Kannapolis after the wedding and stayed there until the conclusion of the racing season. In late 1950, they moved to Daytona Beach, Fla., to be closer to Glenn's family, which was anxiously waiting to meet her. Also, everyone was awaiting the expected March birth of Doris and Fireball's baby.

Doris traveled with Fireball (who had gone professional by this time) at every opportunity. "I didn't like for him to go without me, plus I loved the racing, too. I used to hang around with Margaret Baker (Buddy Baker's mom); Jack Smith's wife, Betty; Speedy Thompson's wife, Jewel, and Pauline Deal. I started scoring in 1952, but I couldn't score for Glenn because NASCAR wouldn't let you score your own husband. They finally allowed it after they realized the wives were going to watch their husbands' cars anyways so they might as well let us score them."

Doris and Glenn, who were still awaiting the birth of their first child, set out from Daytona Beach to Charlotte via automobile in March 1951. They ran across a few problems on the way. "I was nine months pregnant and we were driving to North Carolina," she recalled. "In Savannah, Ga., we got in an automobile accident. We were

(Above) Johnny, the Philip Morris "bellhop," was on hand for this victory at Augusta, Ga., in November 1963.

(Left) Roberts (right) with Ralph Earnhardt (left) and Bobby Isaac: Earnhardt won the NASCAR Sportsman championship in 1956 and passed away in 1973. Isaac won 50 NASCAR Winston Cup poles and 37 races before his death in 1977.

(Below) For a driver who basically ran just "selected" NASCAR Winston Cup races, Roberts was remarkably successful. His record includes 32 victories and 36 poles in just 204 starts.

(Opposite page) People haven't forgotten the fact, either. Doris recently cut the ribbon at the opening of Fireball Speedway Park in Leland, N.C.

all OK but it was a bit scary. When we got to Charlotte, I told my mother that I didn't feel very well. She asked me if I thought I was in labor. I told her that I didn't know because I had never been in labor before. Sure enough … I was … and gave birth to Pamela that night. It was March 11, 1951 … a day I will never forget."

Having a baby certainly changed things from a travel standpoint for Doris, but her love for the sport stayed constant. "It was a little harder when you had children back then at the track because you didn't have any place to go, unless you went in the grandstands or stayed in the infield," she said. "You couldn't do that very well with a little baby. I went every chance I got though."

One of Doris' favorite memories of her years in racing with Fireball was when he won the fourth running of the Daytona 500 in 1962. He drove a Pontiac for team owner Henry "Smokey" Yunick, an eccentric but brilliant mechanic, whose headquarters in Daytona was known as the "Best Damn Garage in Town." Although Fireball's record would include winning the July race there, the Firecracker 400, three times taking victory in NASCAR's biggest event was truly something special. "I will always remember that day as one of my favorite times," Doris said. "I remember Glenn telling me on our second date that he was going to succeed and be a champion in this business. I believed him with all my heart — especially after he won the 500."

Fireball was slated to run the May 1964 event — the World 600 — at Charlotte Motor Speedway. Doris and Pamela, then 13, had decided not to go and stayed at home, in Florida. It turned out to be a day that would haunt Doris for the rest of her life. "Junior Johnson and Ned Jarrett were jockeying for position when they made contact, and Glenn got caught up in their accident," Doris said. "He hit the retaining wall real hard. He had injuries that were life threatening. He was burned all over his body.

"We couldn't get a commercial flight out so some friends took us in their private plane to Charlotte to see him. He was so badly injured and burned. Pamela and I flew back and forth over

GLENN "FIREBALL" ROBERTS

He was a son of small-town Central Florida, had a lightning-fast pitch on the baseball field as a teenager, thought of making engineering his avocation but, instead, ended up becoming stock car racing's first true "superstar."

Edward Glenn Roberts Jr. was born on Jan. 20, 1929 in Tavares, Fla., but grew up in nearby Apopka. He played "organized" ball with the Zellwood Mud Hens, and his prowess on the mound earned him a nickname — "Fireball" — which would stick with him for life.

In 1945, his family relocated to Daytona Beach, Fla., and he enlisted in the Army Air Corps. He was asthmatic, though, and was discharged after 90 days. In 1947, he entered the University of Florida, majoring in mechanical engineering. He ran his first race that March, a Modified event at North Wilkesboro, N.C. Roberts also competed in the first NASCAR-sanctioned event, a 150-miler for Modifieds in February 1948 on a 2.2-mile "Beach-Road" course in Daytona. In early 1950, he dropped out of school to go racing full time.

Roberts, between 1950-55, concentrated on the Modified circuit. He did, however, run 34 NASCAR Winston Cup races, winning one. In '56, Roberts signed on as one of three Ford "factory" team drivers. He entered 33 races and finished in the top five 16 times, including five victories. The following year, Roberts raced for himself, winning eight times, but sold everything at year's end. Driving for car owner Frank Strickland, he switched from Ford to General Motors and won both the 1958 Northern 500 at Trenton, N.J., and Southern 500 at Darlington, S.C., becoming the first NASCAR driver to capture two 500-milers in one season.

By 1961, Roberts had become nationally known, and the following year he made a clean sweep of Daytona by winning the pole for the 500, a 100-mile qualifying race, the Daytona 500 itself and the July Firecracker 250. His last win was appropriately the 1963 Southern 500.

On May 24, 1964, Roberts was involved in a crash in the World 600 at Charlotte Motor Speedway. He received critical burns and died on July 2 in a Charlotte hospital. His NASCAR Winston Cup career spanned 204 races of which he won 32. He was elected to the Stock Car Racing Hall of Fame in 1965.

the next 41 days while he tried hard to survive. He died of blood poisoning and pneumonia. He was only 35. It was such a hard time for Pamela and me. Pamela and I stayed in Daytona for a few years after that. We moved back to North Carolina in 1970. There was so much going on that people just don't know what Pamela and I went through. It was a tough time."

In 1982, Doris moved to Kannapolis, N.C., to be near her mother. She started her own needlecraft shop there for a while before she sold it in 1998. Doris enjoys traveling to some races with friends, who have remained close to her even after all these years. "I have the dearest friends in this sport. I have always enjoyed them all so much," she said.

Even though Doris enjoys attending races, she will still not go to the one track that has plagued her all these years — the place where her husband of almost 14 years lost his life. Fireball Roberts has assumed the status of an icon to many people on both sides of the fence — fans and racers — and has been saluted many times since his death for his contributions to stock car racing. In 1990, he was inducted in to the International Motorsports Hall of Fame. "I am so proud of that honor because I know how hard it is to get voted in to that. He was in the original class of inductees," Doris said. "I am very proud of everything Glenn did. I am proud to still be a part of the sport that he loved and I love, too. My years in racing will always be some of the best times of my life."

Their daughter, Pamela, is married to Rick Trivette and they live in Kannapolis. Doris has a granddaughter in Concord, N.C., and a grandson in Cocoa, Florida.

LINDA RUDD

L inda Carwile was in the third grade when she met Ricky Rudd for the first time. They lived in the same neighborhood, in Chesapeake, Va., and rode on the same school bus. Linda remembered Ricky well because he had a swimming pool in his backyard, which at that time was considered a sign of affluence. "All I really remember about him was he had a pool which was pretty impressive. Not may people had a pool when we were kids," Linda said.

It wasn't until the sixth grade that Linda would form an impression of her future husband. The two were in all the same classes and Linda remembered not being too swept away with this guy named Ricky Rudd. "I did not like him. I thought he was much too sure of himself so I just didn't care for him," she said. "We did not have much to do with each other during that time." This impression didn't change for several years. When Linda found out Ricky had a crush on a girl they both knew, that was leading nowhere, she actually sympathized with him. "He liked a friend of mine and she didn't like him. I felt sorry for Ricky because I had seen a nice side of him through all that and I decided I liked him," Linda noted. "My impression of him changed during that time."

Their first date was shortly after that turnaround of feelings. Linda let Ricky know "I liked him and it went from there." Linda was 16 and Ricky was slightly younger, 15, even though they were in the same grade. "He only lived a block and a half away from me so it was pretty convenient. We went to a movie ... it might have been *Butch Cassidy and The Sundance Kid* ... I think we both knew we liked each other that night."

Ricky and Linda continued to date steadily until they graduated from high school in 1974. Linda was working as an assistant librarian and Ricky was working for his dad, Al Rudd Sr., delivering parts from their junkyard. Ricky "strayed" from time to time to date other women. Linda didn't particularly like the way Ricky treated their relationship. "It was always hard on me when we would break up but then we'd get back together," she said. He even went so far as to give Linda an engagement ring only to call things off again. But finally — on July 6, 1979 — the couple eloped to Elizabeth City, N.C., and became Mr. and Mrs. Ricky Rudd. They bought a house in Chesapeake not to far from where they grew up and faced the future.

Ricky had done a little Go-Kart and motocross around Chesapeake but his real interest was building a stock car using the parts he found in his father's junkyard. Ricky made his NASCAR

(Left) The Rudds alternated between dating steadily and an on-again-off-again relationship before finally deciding to commit their lives to one another in mid-1979. (Opposite page) Life changed somewhat for Linda — but mainly for the better — when Landon Lee came along in August 1994.

Taking in the sites in Tucson, Ariz., in 1999. Despite the rigors of NASCAR Winston Cup Series racing, the Rudds have managed to find "away time" together over the years.

Winston Cup Series debut in 1975 when he ran four races for car owner Bill Champion. The next year, he entered a car owned by his dad in the Daytona 500 but didn't get into the event. As Linda remembered the time, they made the best of it. "Ricky did not make the race so we went to Disney World, instead. We still had fun even though he didn't make it into the race."

Ricky had discovered his love for NASCAR-style racing and fully intended to make it his life's work. He ran races in cars owned by his father for three years and in 1979 got a ride with veteran "independent" team owner Junie Donlavey, who was based in Richmond. Linda quit her job at the library so she could go racing with Ricky. She remembers those early years as being very exciting and sometimes quite tiring. "It was so different from how it is now. We drove everywhere, so we didn't go to the real far-off races. Most of the time we would get up the morning the track opened and leave early enough to drive in before the practice started."

Linda recalls one time in particular that was especially grueling. "Ricky was supposed to fly from Chesapeake to Nashville, Tenn., for a race. There had been an airline strike so when we got to the airport, there was not a ticket for him. I had to drive us really fast back home to pack our bags for us to drive to Nashville. I drove all night in my Datsun B-210 so Ricky could sleep because he had to race the next day. When we got to the track the next morning, I was so tired that I slept in my little car about 90 percent of the day."

In 1983, Ricky's second season with Richard Childress Racing, the Rudds moved to Cornelius, N.C., to be closer to the race shops but kept their permanent home in Chesapeake. "We loved living in Virginia but it just got harder and harder to do with the race shops being in Charlotte," Linda remembered. "We started out by staying in our North Carolina home during the season and Virginia in the off-season, but we knew there might come a time when we would have to move permanently to Cornelius." It was not until after the birth of their son that they would move permanently to the Charlotte area.

Ricky and Linda had almost desperately wanted a family of their own. The couple spent many years praying for a child, but it would be a 15-year wait before they could finally hold

(Left) Ricky grew up near the ocean in Chesapeake, Va., and is passing his love of the water on to his son.

(Below) One of Ricky's favorite photos of Linda, taken sometime during the "Tide years" (1994-99) when he owned his own team.

their baby in their arms. Landon Lee Rudd was born on August 26, 1994. Everyone in the NASCAR family was aware of the years of heartache the Rudds encountered trying to have a child of their own. It had to be one of the most celebrated births in the NASCAR Winston Cup garage area. Landon was the answer to many prayers.

Linda, who had spent many years traveling with her husband, now had a precious baby to tend to. Ricky and Linda had a motor coach and took young Landon with them everywhere. "It was easy for us when Landon was born because by then we had our own airplane and a coach to stay in at the track so we just took him along." It was not until Landon started school that things got a bit more complicated. "Ricky and I knew that once Landon started school we would need to get settled somewhere so we moved to Cornelius so we could be more centralized with racing and he could go to school."

Linda's schedule is somewhat different during the school year. "I usually stay home with Landon during the week and then fly out on the weekends to be with Ricky. Landon goes about half the time with us. The other time he stays at home," she said.

(Above) "No, son, this isn't a race car!" Ricky and Landon rode together at Disney World in 1998.

(Right) Linda and Ricky got away together for awhile on a trip to Cancun, Mexico, in 1997.

(Opposite page) It's siesta time for the men of the Rudd household in 1995!

RICKY RUDD

Born on Sept. 12, 1956 in Chesapeake, Va., Ricky Rudd has been a charter member of the NASCAR Winston Cup Series for over 25 years.

Rudd started racing motocross and Go-Karts as a youngster, but it was the fact that his dad, Al Rudd Sr., owned an auto salvage yard that piqued his interest in stock car racing. He made his first NASCAR Winston Cup start on March 2, 1975 in the Carolina 500 at Rockingham, N.C. He qualified Bill Champion's Ford 26th fastest, ran 450 of 492 laps and finished 11th. Rudd ran 42 races in cars owned by his father from 1976-78 and captured the series' Rookie of the Year award in '77 with 10 top-10 finishes in 25 starts.

Rudd ran the 1979 season for fellow Virginian Junie Donlavey but returned to cars owned by his dad in 1980. He ran 13 races and he caught the eye of racing's power players by qualifying second fastest at Charlotte in October and finishing fourth. That was part of the reason he was picked up by the prominent DiGard Racing Co., team in 1981.

In one season with DiGard, Rudd won three poles (his first came on April 24 at Martinsville, Va.), he finished second three times, fourth three times, had 17 top-10 finishes in 31 starts and was sixth in points. That was good enough for Richard Childress, who needed a new driver. Rudd was winless in 1982 but his first career win (and the first for Childress Racing) came on June 5, 1983 at Riverside, Calif. He won once more for Childress before moving to the Bud Moore team in 1984, where he spent four seasons. He raced for drag racer/NASCAR Winston Cup team owner Kenny Bernstein in 1988-89 and ran for Hendrick Motorsports 1990-93.

Rudd formed his own team in 1994 but when he lost his sponsor and couldn't find a replacement, he sold out at the end of 1999 to Robert Yates Racing — for whom he agreed to drive. Rudd went winless in 2000 but the following year won twice, for a career total of 22 victories. From 1983-98, he won at least once per season, a streak of 16 years.

Ricky and Linda, who are both pranksters, love to share stories with Landon about each other. For instance, Landon once asked Ricky what it was like for him when he was in school. His parents laughed as they shared a story about their high-school years when Linda had a crush on Ricky. He was leaning back in a chair combing his hair when his chair slipped and down Ricky went to the floor, red face and all.

Linda giggled at Landon's response when someone asked him if he wants to race someday. His response is a simple, "My momma wont let me." Linda admitted that her son does talk about his future at times but seems to be interested in being an aircraft pilot. "I'd like for him to see what all is out there in the world. I hope he does not want to race but if he does, of course, Ricky and I would support him but I hope he doesn't."

The Rudds have spent many years in racing. Although the sport's been good to them, Linda looks forward to the day they can rest and spend more time at home. "I'm sure Ricky will stay involved in racing," she said. "We are still bouncing around the different options when he does retire. I want to be able to volunteer at Landon's school, I do some (volunteer work) now, but I would like to do more. I just really want to stay home and be normal. I want to take a deep breath and go, 'Whew!'"

ANN SCHRADER

*T*he woman who ended up being race driver Ken Schrader's wife decided as a teenager that she wanted to become a nurse when she got out of high school. The former Ann Pokrefke described her childhood (she was one of five kids) in St. Louis as something between a "Norman Rockwell setting" and that wacky clan portrayed in the popular **Family Vacation** trilogy of movie comedies starring Chevy Chase and Beverly D'Angelo.

"I grew up a little Polish girl in a good old American home," Ann said. "I had this great 55-year-old chemistry teacher that really got to me. He convinced me that nursing was a good safe route to go as far as always having a job. I was definitely looking to the future. It was more that than a Florence Nightingale type of thing. I ended up realizing that I really enjoyed it."

Born in February 1957, Ann graduated from high school in 1975 and went straight to nursing school. After getting her registered nurse's license in 1978, she got a job at a large health-care facility in St. Louis. It was during that time that Ann was briefly married to a longtime boyfriend, who also raced at the local track near her home. Ann and her first husband befriended another young married couple, Mr. And Mrs. Kenny Schrader.

"Kenny and I were married at the same time to different people," she explained. "How funny is that? We all would go to the races and just have a good time. My husband at the time raced at the same track where Kenny did, so we all knew each other and enjoyed hanging out with everyone. Kenny and his wife started having problems and later divorced. My husband and I kind of took Kenny in. He was lonely so he would hang out with us a lot. It was as innocent as innocent could be between us."

While Ann's story sounds something like a TV sit-com, it's true. She and her husband were having domestic problems and later divorced. By 1981, she was working as a nursing supervisor, had her life in order and was content. Then, Ken came across her business card and decided to call. "We met again very innocently," she recalled. "We would meet at Denny's and just talk and talk. We immediately hit it off. We were both surprised at how we liked to be together.

"It kind of got funny from here. He was dating a girl who ended up dumping him at Christmas. He would come over and hang out because I guess he didn't want to spend the holidays by himself. I had a friend's wedding to go to in December '81 and didn't particularly want to go by myself. I asked if he would go with me as a

(Left) The Schraders in the doorway of their new mobile home, in 1986, in North Carolina: Ann called the manufacturer of the building her "hero." (Opposite page) The Schraders "at home" in 1997: Dorothy Lynn was around 7 and Sheldon Bradley was about 18 months old.

friend. He said, 'Yes, if you go with me to this banquet I have in January.' So he went with me to the wedding and in January I went with him to the racing banquet. I ended up sitting with the parents of the girl who had dumped Kenny before Christmas. I didn't realize it at first. That was an interesting night!

"From that point on we knew we were attracted to each other. He was a lot of fun and I found myself really wanting to be with him more and more. By Easter of that year we were pretty serious. He kept doing stuff that he would have never done before in other relationships. He would go with me and my friends to do silly things like ice skating. Kenny had lived in St. Louis all his life and he had never ice-skated. We had a lot of fun doing lots of different things. I found out he was so sweet and quite charming."

Kenny and Ann dated for the next two years while he was racing open-wheel cars with the United States Auto Club (USAC) and suddenly they decided to break things off. She said things had been fine but for some reason he started acting "wiggy" about the relationship. In effect, Ann told him he could live his own life, but she wasn't wasting her time. End of relationship.

"We were apart for two weeks while he got his head straight. When we talked about getting back together, I showed him a calendar and said, 'Here, pick a day. If you are on the fence, go one way or the other because I am not wasting my time while you decide.'"

Kenny made it clear that he was not going to live his life without Ann. They married at high noon on Nov. 13, 1984 in St. Louis. The ceremony was held at the Church of the Open Word, and the newlyweds had fun telling their friends the nuptials took place at the "Church of What's Happening Now." It was a quick wedding because Ann had to get back to work and Ken had to leave the following day for a race in California. Some honeymoon!

"Kenny was racing all over the country at that time. I would work during the week and then drive all night to see him race on the weekends," Ann said. "He would get some bad phone bills from calling me from all over. He didn't always have the money to pay them. He'd run up a thousand-dollar phone bill. The phone company would get ready to cut him off. Then he'd win a race so he would pay the bill plus some for credit for the next month."

In 1986 Kenny and Ann decided it was time to move to North Carolina. They put their house up for rent in St. Louis, just in case they ever wanted to go back home, and still own it today. They moved into a mobile home on the five acres right outside of Charlotte they had recently purchased. Ann called the manufacturer of their residence, Oakwood Homes, her "hero."

(Above) Every so often Ann does get her husband to slow down long enough to enjoy their home in North Carolina. She, however, doesn't see her life as being especially frantic.

(Left) Because of his standing in the local community, Ken is called upon to participate in school programs. The entire family came along for this "show-and-tell" event in 1995.

(Above) Christmas 2001 — a family portrait.

(Opposite page) Sheldon gets a taste of life in Dad's "office;" Dorothy snuggles up with her favorite M&M's!

Everything was done over the phone, and "they set us up in 784 square feet of wonder. We brought our furniture and moved in. It was great."

Ann took a nursing position at Carolinas Medical Center in Charlotte shortly after setting up house. "I loved my job there," she said. "I worked with 'preemie' babies (premature births). I worked as long as I could with Kenny racing. I was only working four days a month before I left there to travel with Kenny and start our own family."

Ann, who has never been at a loss for conversation, made many friends in the sport — perhaps more than her husband. "It was funny because I knew more people in NASCAR than Kenny did. I got to be friends with all of them. Some of my best girlfriends were Ricé Speed (wife of former NASCAR Winston Cup driver Lake Speed) and Marcia Parsons (wife of driver Phil Parsons). We all ran together and had a fun time doing it."

Ann and Kenny had wanted a family of their own but like many other racing families, it didn't happen as fast as they would have liked. It took five years for Dorothy to come along.

"It's a common problem with race car drivers," Ann said. "The question is, could the high temperatures that these guys drive in for long periods of time damage their baby-making capabilities? I think it does." Kenny and Ann finally got the baby they'd wanted when Dorothy Lynn came into the world on New Year's Eve 1989. Their second child, Sheldon Bradley, was born on Dec. 19, 1995.

"I think I was prepared to travel with kids to the track. I learned to be a track mule," Ann said. "I knew Kenny would not be able to help me because of his schedule, so I kept pretty busy hustling kids. I have to say a big thank you to women like Lynda Petty and Judy Allison who worked so hard all those years before things were like they are now. They are the real heroes."

Families like the Schraders who have been around racing for many years have certainly been through difficult situations. In 2001, Kenny and Ann experienced one of the toughest when their friend, Dale Earnhardt, died in a last-lap crash in the Daytona 500. Kenny and Sterling Marlin were also in the fatal wreck but were not its cause.

"Dale's death was hard on all of us, especially Kenny," Ann said. "He was the first one to the car after Dale crashed and didn't come back from the infield care center right away ... so I knew something was wrong. Kenny felt blessed that he was there with him when he died. That is how we looked at the tragedy, but it did change us. I think it made me more aware of my family and life. We all know how we love our families but sometimes I think we need to remind ourselves to live today to the fullest because we might not have tomorrow. Kenny and I look at life as maybe more fragile now. It is a shame it takes someone's death to remind us of that. We were pretty anchored through the tragedy so I guess we did OK under the circumstances."

Ann is very involved in the Motor Racing Outreach ministry, as well as the NASCAR Winston Cup Racing Wives Auxiliary where she serves as president. "I think MRO does a bang-up job with the youth and the whole NASCAR family," she said. "They help all of us. I don't think my life is harder being married to a race car driver. I think we all have our struggles in life; it's how you look at it that matters. I look at it as my family is blessed to have what we have in each other and the friendships in our lives. We have our health, what more can you ask for?"

Kenny is approaching the age where thoughts of retirement usually crop up. Ann, however, doesn't see that anytime soon. "Kenny will race 'till he can't compete anymore," she said. "If he is physically capable of racing, no matter what his age, he will race. But when that time comes ... we will definitely stay in the sport. We love it too much. I personally would have fun in a school setting. I wouldn't mind maybe teaching nursing. I think I'll teach in my next life."

KEN SCHRADER

St. Louis native Ken Schrader, who celebrated his 46th birthday on May 29, may not have won a NASCAR Winston Cup Series race in over 10 years, but he is certainly one of the circuit's most energetic drivers.

Schrader said that his interest in racing came as a kid when his father bought a Go-Kart, tethered it to a pole he'd put in their backyard, put his son in the little machine and let him run as fast as he could. Schrader joked that he'd been "going in circles" ever since.

Schrader started racing when he was 16. Although he won the United States Auto Club stock car division Rookie of the Year award in 1980, being from the Midwest he gravitated toward open-wheel competition. He has 33 victories in Midgets, Sprints and Silver Crown cars, and won the USAC Silver Crown championship in 1982 and the Sprint Car title the following season.

Ford Motor Co. executives had their eye on Schrader and suggested he give the NASCAR Winston Cup Series a try. Veteran "independent" team owner (and later the series' pace car driver), the late Elmo Langley, gave Schrader a shot in 1984. He rented one of his Fords to Schrader for three races and then paid the bills himself for two more. Schrader then signed on with Junie Donlavey's Ford team and raced with him for three seasons (1985-87) before switching alliances to Chevrolet and Hendrick Motorsports in 1988. His first NASCAR Winston Cup Series victory came that year — at Talladega, Ala. — his second came the next year and he won twice more for Hendrick in 1991.

Schrader left Hendrick at the end of 1996, drove for Andy Petree Racing for three seasons and then moved to his present ride — MB2 Motorsports in 2000.

Schrader also owns his own team — Schrader Racing in Concord, N.C. — where he fields entries on a variety of circuits. He also fits as many non-NASCAR Winston Cup events into his schedule as possible and has an ownership stake in a Missouri dirt track.

ANGELA SKINNER

*A*ngela Edwards was born and raised in Fairborn, Ohio, a suburb of Dayton. She had an older sister, 13 years her senior, whose husband loved racing. As a child she would sit and watch the races never dreaming that one day she would marry a driver herself. "It was funny because I would watch the races because I had to. There was nothing else to do," she said. "We laugh about it now."

"Angie," as most of her friends call her, had her heart set on being a television personality or a movie star when she grew up. She attended Capital College in Columbus, Ohio, where she studied broadcasting and acting. In 1994 she earned her degree in television and broadcasting with acting as a minor. She then set out to put her education to work at WHOK — "K95 Country" — in Columbus as an account executive in "nontraditional marketing." The job would lead to her first meeting with race driver Mike Skinner.

"I was working for a radio station that was a CBS affiliate. I worked in sales and marketing, which was putting together different promotions and things of that nature," she said. "We discovered that after you sell out radio spots, we had to make more money for the station. That's where nontraditional marketing pays big. You create a big event — concert, race, etc. — and find companies to sponsor it. We found that NASCAR was really hitting hard in our region. We also became partners with local stock car and NHRA tracks. We sold out our first NASCAR event, and they put me in charge to create a new one the following year. I ended up booking John Andretti, Sterling Marlin, Jerry Nadeau, Chad Little and (crew chief) Jeff Hammond. The event took place at an NHRA strip near Columbus, and we had the Cup drivers drag racing against an NHRA team — and the NASCAR guys won!

"After that I was invited to Michigan Speedway. I was given a garage pass so I was able to meet a lot of people while I was working on my different projects. I convinced the radio station I was working for to let me cover NASCAR on Sundays. I would go around and get one-liners from the drivers for my reports."

As a reporter, Angie naturally got to meet racing people of all descriptions, many whom became her friends. One was Donnie "Fat Boy" Epling, who drove Mike's motorhome. "Fat Boy chased me down one day to try to get me to meet Mike. He said, 'Come on, you've got to meet Skinner.' Finally at Martinsville, Va., in 1999 I went over to meet him. He had a lot going on," Angie recalled. "Mike showed a friend of mine and me his motorcoach, and we all

Angela Edwards' college education and subsequent job at least indirectly led to her meeting her future husband.

just talked for a little while. I remember thinking he was cute and quite charming. I was a bit surprised by my reaction to him. Oddly enough he started flirting with my friend who was with me. They even went out on a date after that. I actually got a little jealous but didn't know why.

"After he went out with her, I ran in to him again. He asked me for my cell phone number and I got his. It was kind of funny how it all worked out because he called me five minutes after he got my number and asked, 'Did I wait long enough to call you?' I found out later, he was using reverse psychology by going out with my friend. It worked!"

Angie and Mike hit it off and found that they had a lot in common except for maybe the age difference. "I was a bit concerned about the age difference in Mike and myself. I kept thinking he is 15 years older than me. But at the same time it felt like I was where I was supposed to be. I am a firm believer in everything happening for a reason, and, no doubt Mike happened for a reason."

154

Mike and Angie continued to see each other on the weekends. She was still working while he was racing. When the weekends were over she would go home to Ohio and he would head back to Florida. "It got to where I didn't want to be away from him and he felt the same about me. I used to hate for the weekend to end," she said. "I remember we were getting ready to go to California one weekend to race, and he said, 'You are not working this weekend. You are going to be my girlfriend.' That was it for me. Not age or anything else mattered to me anymore."

After a courtship of about a year, Angela and Mike were married in November 2000. They then moved from North Carolina to Florida.

Angela said she wanted more from life as a racer's wife than getting "her nails done every week." Hence, she began tending to her husband's business affairs. The arrangement seems to be working for both.

One year after they met at the Martinsville track, Mike asked Angie to be his bride. They were married on Nov. 25, 2000. At first they resided in Greensboro, N.C., but found they loved Daytona Beach so much they bought a home there. Maybe he didn't carry her across the threshold, but when she saw the sign Mike had place over the front door — "Mike and Angie's Place" — her heart melted.

Angie, who had always worked and enjoyed doing so, felt that she was competent enough to run Mike's office and handle his business ventures. She assumed responsibility for his day-to-day affairs. Her responsibilities include souvenir approvals, arranging her husband's busy appearance schedule, pitching endorsements and developing Mike's web site for his fans.

"This is how I like it. I am happy when I am working and staying busy," she said. "Mike trusts me to oversee his dealings. Who better to take care of these things than his own wife, who has all his best interests at heart — and mine, for that matter? We are a team in everything we do. I'm not in this to get my nails done every week. I need more."

Being the wife of a well-known athlete has both its advantages and certainly its disadvantages. As Angie found out in July 2001, the toughest times are those spent at home, away from the track when everyone else is on the scene. Early in the inaugural Tropicana 400 at the new Chicagoland Speedway, a tire on Mike's Richard Childress Racing Chevrolet deflated and sent him crashing into the wall. Mike sustained a mild concussion and broken left ankle. Surgeons repaired the fracture, but Mike missed the next four races. He came back and entered the following five events but was not feeling quite right. Instead of putting himself, and others, at risk, he told Richard he was stepping out of the car for good. His association with the team was ending anyway, and Mike felt it would be better to spend time gathering his strength for his new assignment with Morgan-McClure Motorsports in 2002.

"I knew the risk would always be there for Mike to get hurt. I didn't realize all the other things that go along with that, like the rehab, and the mental obstacles to overcome," said Angie. "It's so hard to love someone like I love Mike and watch them go through what we went through in 2001. Mike was leaving one team, going to another, and on top of everything else he needed surgery. Every week was a struggle before the tough decisions were made. I am so thankful that we are where we are now and that Mike is back in the car, feeling good about what he is doing. The hardest part of this profession for a driver is when, for some reason, they can't drive. The hardest part for a wife is seeing them so unhappy. They are miserable when they can't race."

Mike, who had previously been married, has two older children, Jamie, who is 24, and Dustin is 17. "I have a real good relationship with Jamie and Dustin. They are great to me and I enjoy them. My mother is like a grandmother to them. We are blessed in that we all get along," Angie said.

Angie has settled quite comfortably into her role of a driver's wife. At first, however, she worried about how her peer group would accept her and admitted to feeling awkward and out of place. She learned, though, that, as is true with life in general, it just takes a little time to make new friends and form common bonds.

"I met Linda McReynolds, Robin Dallenbach and Diane Bodine, who were really great to me, and I really liked them," she said. "Once I got to know these girls I felt a lot more at home. It just takes time. It is more like you almost have to prove yourself to everyone. It was nothing intended to be mean to me by anyone but a hard lesson nonetheless. I love having my girlfriends and hanging out with them because I feel that no one else can really relate to what I go through each week like another driver's wife can. But, at the end of the day my best friend is always Mike."

Angie is usually at every race. Before every start, she makes a point of writing her husband a short note. It's an endearing routine — one that he deeply appreciates. "It's something I started awhile back. I'll put a note in his shoe or in his firesuit or somewhere that he can read before he goes out to race," Angie said. "I write different things. Sometimes I just say, 'I love you.' Other times it might be a note of encouragement. It just depends what has gone on throughout the weekend. Growing up, I always dreamed of getting married one day. I always wondered who it would be or where I would meet him. It is amazing to me that I found someone like Mike. I'm so glad that I did. I really and truly feel blessed to get to be with my best friend, my husband, every day. I am so blessed."

MIKE SKINNER

For Mike Skinner, racing started out as a hobby. Born on June 28, 1957 in Ontario, Calif., he grew up in the small town of Susanville. He started racing on the local short track there and after winning three championships wondered if he had the stuff to make the sport his living.

He got the necessary push from his first wife, who insisted he either move to North Carolina (which he did in 1983) and race or forget about it. After cutting his teeth on short tracks in the Carolinas and Virginia, he ran 10 NASCAR Winston Cup races for four small teams between 1986-94 and caught the eye of leading team owner Richard Childress. When the NASCAR Craftsman Truck Series made its debut in 1995, Childress assembled a team and gave the driving job to Skinner. The Californian then won the inaugural truck series event at Phoenix, Ariz., on Feb. 5 and went on to win the championship. The following season he finished third in points and in two seasons had scored 16 wins and 15 poles in 44 races.

Skinner also ran five NASCAR Winston Cup races for Childress in '96, and in '97 went full time on the circuit as a teammate to Dale Earnhardt. He was the only rookie driver to win the poles for both races at Daytona International Speedway in the same year. He finished in the top 10 three times, earned over $950,000 and was named Rookie of the Year. He also won a special "demonstration" race in Suzuka, Japan.

Skinner returned to Japan the following year and captured another "demonstration" event, this time narrowly beating Jeff Gordon at the Twin Ring oval at Motegi. In the regular season, he finished in the top 10 nine times and was 21st in points. Despite a broken shoulder blade he sustained at a race in Texas, he finished the 1999 season with 14 top-10 finishes and a career high 10th place in points.

Skinner missed several races in 2001 because of injury and after opting to have corrective surgery, resigned from Childress' team before the end of the year. He then inked a contract to race with Morgan-McClure Motorsports and sponsor Kodak film in 2002.

PAT SPENCER

P *at Perey was one of four children of John
and Barbara Perey, all daughters, and
grew up in the little town of Berwick, Pa. Her
family's claim to fame was her grandfather, John,
who, in 1907, invented the "Perey Turnstile" you
walk through at ballparks, coliseums and race
tracks. While he sold his interest in the company
in 1941, it still operates today in Connecticut
and New York.*

"There was nothing special about my childhood," Pat noted. "We did all the normal stuff. I had my friends and my boyfriends but just the normal stuff." That is until one of those friends, Justine "Teenie" Spencer, introduced Pat to her brother, Jimmy.

"I was best friends with Jimmy's sister. She was my age and we were together all the time. She used to talk about Jimmy, but I was dating someone else so I was not really interested in him," Pat explained. "I went with Teenie one day to their house and Jimmy was there. I didn't pay any attention to him at all. I remember meeting him, but that was about it. Teenie told me later that Jimmy had asked about me and was interested in me. My boyfriend and I broke up soon after that, so Teenie asked Jimmy if he wanted to take me out. He said yes, so we went out the next night."

Pat was a high school junior and Jimmy a senior when they went on their first date in 1975. She remembered they went to a movie at a local drive-in theater and "had a lot of fun." The relationship then got "serious fast," and the matchmaker in this story, Teenie, didn't seem to mind at all. The following year Jimmy started racing Late Model class cars at Port Royal (Pa.) Speedway, a half-mile dirt track. "I had never been to a race so it was all new to me, but I did like it," Pat said. "I got real involved with his racing because it was what he did. I got so involved that I would work on his parts truck and sell racing parts during the race. We would buy parts and put them on the truck and I would work in the truck while Jimmy raced."

Pat graduated from high school in '76 and went off to college in Philadelphia while Jimmy stayed in Berwick to pursue his racing career. "I'd ride the bus home every weekend to see him or he would come to Philadelphia to be with me. It was tiring and very hard for us to be apart."

Pat completed one semester, left the big city and moved back home to be closer to Jimmy. She enrolled in nearby Luzerne (County) Community College and after two years graduated with a business degree. The couple put her education to good use, as they

(Left) Pat Spencer knew nothing about auto racing, but that all changed when she met Jimmy. Their early years together were hard but success has brought them security. (Opposite page) According to Pat, she and Jimmy got married out of necessity. They were both broke and even had to curtail their racing for awhile.

Because they both came from loving families, Pat and Jimmy wanted children of their own. James was born in 1986 and Katrina came along about two years later. The pets are important members of the Spencer household, too.

purchased a car lot to finance Jimmy's racing. "I did title work during the day and cleaned the cars up at night while Jimmy worked on his race cars, sometimes all night," she said. "We were open from 9 a.m. to 9 p.m. but closed early on Saturday to go racing. The tracks were relatively close so we could usually get there pretty quickly."

Pat and Jimmy had been going together for six years and had talked a bit about marriage, but as Pat remembers it wasn't a major topic of discussion. "I never remember him really asking me to marry him," she said. "We were racing and were dead broke, so we had to get married to survive. We got married in 1981 and moved into a trailer outside of Berwick that we bought from his parents. We had to stop racing and just sell used cars until we got enough money to race again. Our business grew and we started getting a lot of repeat customers. Our customers loved Jimmy." Later that year, they finally had enough money to start racing again, as Jimmy was adamant about becoming a professional driver.

Pat and Jimmy also were determined to have a family, which they did with the birth of their son, James, in May 1986, and daughter Katrina in May 1988. "Katrina was only two

At home on the lake: Moving north of Charlotte was quite a change from living in an apartment in Kannapolis, N.C.

months old when I started dragging her to all of Jimmy's races," Pat said. "I'd keep her in the van or sit in the grandstands with all her toys and my diaper bag. It was really hard at times, especially because I had two children to drag around, but it was fun, too."

The Spencers relocated to North Carolina in May 1988 so Jimmy could start competing in the NASCAR Busch Series. He'd gone on a house-hunting expedition in April and found an apartment in Kannapolis. About a year later, Jimmy got a phone call that opened the door into the Winston Cup Series, his goal all along. "It was during the June Dover (Del.) race when Buddy Baker called to talk to Jimmy about Winston Cup," Pat recalled. "Jimmy hung up, thinking it was a joke, but when it turned out to be Buddy, it was pretty funny."

Jimmy and Pat made a permanent transition to Winston Cup racing when Jimmy ran 17 races for Baker-Schiff Racing in 1989. As always, Pat continued to travel with her husband, only now life had become a bit more complex. "Things were so different for me," she said. "It took a little getting used to, but I knew it was what Jimmy always wanted. I always like to be with Jimmy when he is racing, but it did get harder when the kids got in school." In 1993, Jimmy and Pat bought a house on Lake Norman north of Charlotte where they enjoy jet ski-ing and other outdoor activities with their children. Their only wish is to spend less time away from their home and more time enjoying it.

Pat is a very spiritual person, who feels her faith is the backbone of her marriage and her life. She unabashedly admits to praying for her children, friends and every competitor when the green flag drops. "My faith is important to my family and me," she said. "We have Bible study at our house for adults and for MRO (Motor Racing Outreach) youth, which is a very important part of our lives. I get nervous on race day so I pray about it. I am more scared of head injury than anything, I think."

(Above) The Spencers enjoy living on Lake Norman (the house sits on the waterfront) but only wish they could spend more time there and less on the road.

(Right) What the future holds for Pat and Jimmy depends, at least partially, on the lives their children choose. Katrina might opt for college, while James has already gotten his feet wet in racing.

Pat and Jimmy's son, Jim, now 16, has done a little racing of his own, competing in amateur events, but Pat feels he should experience his youth to the fullest before he seriously gets involved in the sport. "It's scary thinking about Jimmy wanting to race, but more than anything we want him to enjoy being a kid," she said. "His dad told him he needs to do other things, too, while he is young. If he still wants to race when he's older, then we will support him because we want him to be in the safest equipment possible."

Pat's seen many changes in racing since becoming part of it — some good and some not so good. "Racing used to be fun but now it is all business," she noted. "We used to all have full

time jobs and race because we loved it. We didn't have much money, but it was good racing. I remember not too many years ago being able to hop in your car and drive out of the track when the race was over but not now. Television and media exposure is much different, too."

What does the future hold for Pat and her husband? Realistically, Jimmy, now 45, probably has several more competitive seasons in front of him before retirement, but the verdict is still out on what life after racing will hold for the family. "We've talked about staying involved in Busch Series racing as team owners, but I don't see a Winston Cup car because the costs are almost beyond our comprehension," she said. "I guess it also depends on what the kids want. Katrina might want to go to college or she might own her own race team. Who knows?

"I've built so many friendships at the track. They are our neighbors ... my family. My 'real' neighbors at home I don't know well at all. I cannot imagine what it would be like without the excitement of racing with all its ups and downs. I wouldn't know what else to do. Maybe I need a little chaos in my life. I don't know, but for 27 years racing has been a part of my life. I don't know anything else. I do love it."

JIMMY SPENCER

Jimmy Spencer kind of had an idea what he wanted to do in life when he was 15 and snuck into the garage area at Pocono (Pa.) Raceway to meet his hero — A.J. Foyt.

Spencer, a native of Berwick, Pa., and born on Feb. 15, 1957, picked up his interest in racing from his dad, Ed, who also raced cars. Spencer began racing at Port Royal (Pa.) Speedway in the Late Model Division but switched to the more popular open-wheel Modifieds and was the Rookie of the Year at Shangri-La Speedway, in Owego, N.Y., in 1979. He got better and faster, picked up the nickname, "Mr. Excitement," because of his no-holds-barred driving style and claimed the NASCAR national Modified Series championship in 1986 and again in '87.

Switching to a full-time gig in the Busch Series in 1988, Spencer won three races the next year, two in 1992 and through 2001 had recorded 11 victories.

Spencer caught the break he was searching for — a ride in the Winston Cup Series — in 1989 when he ran 17 races for a team co-owned by former driver Buddy Baker and clothing company owner Danny Schiff. He ran 17 races and finished three times in the top 10. In '90, he spent the season with a team owned by Rod Osterlund (who gave the late Dale Earnhardt his start), but the team folded and Spencer moved to a team headed by Travis Carter in 1992.

Spencer raced for Bobby Allison Motorsports in 1993, finishing a career-high 12th in Winston Cup points. But it was the 1994 season with the Junior Johnson and Associates team where he was most successful. He won the Pepsi 400 in July at Daytona Beach, Fla., and followed that up with a stirring victory at Talladega, Ala.

Spencer spent the next seven seasons with Haas-Carter Motorsports without winning and accepted an offer to drive for Chip Ganassi Racing and team up with driver Sterling Marlin in 2002.

BUNNY TURNER HALL

*S*he was a nineteen-year-old bank teller living in the largest city in both Carolinas. He was a forty-one-year-old flamboyant entrepreneur / race car driver ... a real honest-to goodness Renaissance man. What could these two people from different worlds have in common? On the surface one would think not much, but as the two would find out, their love for each other would be a common link — one that would last a lifetime.

In 1968, Carolyn "Bunny" Vance spent her days working as a teller for The Bank of Charlotte. The urban setting was a far cry from her birthplace of Spruce Pine, N.C., a place of perhaps a couple of thousand souls hidden in the mountains of western North Carolina. The daughter of Maude J. and Virgil Vance, she was the "baby" of eight children. In fact, that's the reason for her nickname.

"One of my brothers, Danny, was raising baby rabbits when I was born," she recalled. "When they brought me home from the hospital, Danny said to my mother, 'Mama, look at the baby rabbit — the bunny.' The name took. I still consider Danny to be my clone. We're pretty tight."

At the bank, Bunny had her regular customers, who came in frequently, and one in particular stood out, a handsome businessman by the name of Curtis Morton Turner. "All I knew about him was that he had a driving school," she said of her first reaction to this intriguing stranger. "He would always come to me to take care of his business. He came in every day. One day he wanted me to cash a check that was in the amount of $7,400. We were not supposed to cash any checks for more than $25 without making sure the funds were there. I just cashed it without checking on the funds and he asked for my phone number, all at the same time."

Curtis was persistent in his pursuit of Bunny and he showed it by sending her flowers at the bank daily, along with the many phone calls he made in hopes of persuading her to go out with him. Bunny was living with three girls at the time, and all of them kept pushing her to give this fellow a chance. They could not understand her concern over the age difference.

Bunny finally gave in and agreed to go out with this dashing and beguiling "older man," who was born in Virginia in 1924.

Bunny remembers their first date as something out of a fairy tale: "He pulled up to my house in a big black Cadillac. All the other guys I had dated drove old beat-up cars. I thought to myself, 'What in the world am I doing?' He drove us to the airport where he had his personal airplane waiting on us. We got in it to look around ... or I thought to look around ... and he told me that he had a surprise for me. I looked at him and said, 'I am not flying in that airplane.' He told me to just trust him."

(Left) Today, Bunny resides in Christiansburg, Va., with her husband, Tommy Hall. (Opposite page) Over three decades ago, though, she was married to one of the most flamboyant — and unforgettable — drivers to ever compete in any form of the sport.

Curtis was an accomplished pilot, and he flew himself and his date to Atlanta for a night in the big city. There was a limousine waiting for them when they arrived that whisked them to the Peachtree Hotel in downtown Atlanta. "He gave me my own room and was such a gentleman," recalled Bunny of Curtis and their arrival at the hotel.

Bunny, who had no idea that she would be gone overnight didn't have a thing to wear. Always the gentleman, Curtis took her shopping for clothes and other items she might need. Afterward, the two had a beautiful dinner. Curtis ended the evening with a gentle kiss on her forehead that went through her body like a bolt of lightning. "I had never felt that way before," said Bunny about the tender kiss. This was a night that Bunny would never forget.

The next day when they arrived back in Charlotte, Curtis took Bunny home. When he walked her to her door he turned to her and said, "I am going to marry you, little girl."

Bunny was just as much infatuated with him as he was with her at this point. She just didn't know it yet, nor was she willing to admit

it to anyone — not even herself. Then came the third date and Curtis came to pick Bunny up in a green Corvette. He somehow knew about Bunny's love for the sporty Chevrolet. She asked him who's 'Vette it was and he announced, "It's yours." Bunny was shocked by his generosity and told him boldly, "I cannot accept this car. You must be crazy." Curtis was crazy ... crazy about her and wouldn't take no for an answer.

Curtis wouldn't accept the word no in his vocabulary with regard to Bunny being his wife, either. The two were wed in Chester, South Carolina in December 1968 just nine months after their first date.

Bunny's mother was concerned about her marrying someone so much older than she was. She asked her daughter one day, "What will you do when he is eighty years old and in a wheelchair?" Bunny replied, "Push him!"

The couple's life was like a whirlwind from the very first. Curtis was in the timber business where he bought and sold big tracts of lumber. He also had a love for racing, as he was running a driving school and racing competitively himself.

Bunny's memories from those early days of their marriage are probably some of the most special. One night in particular when Bunny and Curtis were living in Roanoke, Va., they had her brother, Danny, and his wife over to spend the night. The next morning the Turners were to travel to Harland, Ky. Curtis had an option on a large tract of timber and wanted to check it out first. The area, however, was beset by labor problems and the town was actually under

(Left) While Bunny enjoyed the hustle and bustle of living with Curtis Turner, her life today is a bit more subdued.

(Below) That's not to say she's a recluse, though, as she and Tommy enjoy socializing and meeting other "racing folk" like Liz Allison.

At one time, Curtis Jr., thought of pursuing his late father's profession — racing. He, however, chose to devote his life to his wife and children and pursued a career that would keep him closer to home.

marshal law. To be on the "safe side," Curtis insisted Bunny bring along a .38-caliber pistol, which had been left on a nightstand by their bed.

As Bunny recalls the mishap: "Things were quiet at night. I was in the bed with Curtis and reached over him to get something when my hand slipped and hit the pistol Curtis had bought me, which caused it to go off. I scared everybody to death. My brother must have thought we shot someone. It was so funny at the time. It scared Curtis to death, too. Curtis thought I had shot myself, and I thought he had shot me. My ears rang for a week.

"Harland was a wild place at the time. When we got there, the only place to eat was the local VFW hall. When we arrived there for dinner, even the women were packing guns!"

Bunny remembers her days as a driver's wife somewhat differently from the majority of the wives of that era. For instance, many times she would watch her husband race from a VIP booth far from the infield parking lots where the other wives were exiled. She was friendly with the corporate types because of Curtis' business dealings so she never had a chance to really meet other racers' wives. In fact, she frankly admits that she and her spouse had a lifestyle that was quite removed from most other couples in the sport.

"Curtis and I flew in our plane to all the races whereas everyone else drove so I never had the opportunity to get to know everyone like I wish I could have," she said. "Most of the time we would fly but if we drove, Curtis would pick me up in my pajamas in a limousine and we would drive all night to a race. I was so spoiled."

Curtis had been involved in many "deals" over the years, but one was particularly important to him. He wanted to build a new auto-racing track that would outshine anything else in existence. He didn't approach the idea lightly, as he and a partner, O. Bruton Smith, pooled their resources to construct what is now Lowe's Motor Speedway outside of Charlotte. The 1.5-mile track opened in 1960 but in about a year went into bankruptcy, and the two partners were forced out. Hence, this latest project was, in effect, an ongoing work in progress — but unfortunately one that would never come to pass.

Curtis (who, in 1998, was named one of NASCAR's 50 greatest drivers of all time) had decided to retire from racing as a driver to focus more on family and his businesses. There was also something else: The couple was elated in the fact that they were expecting their first child in late October 1970. Hence, Curtis was planning on making the announcement of his retirement at the end of the '70 racing season.

October 4 was not a usual day for Bunny. She woke up that morning with a knot in her stomach. Being eight and half months pregnant, she thought the tenseness might be from her condition, but somehow the feeling would just not go away.

"Curtis had been real busy working on the new track plans and had just gotten home from a meeting the night before," Bunny recollected of the day's events. "He decided to take a trip for the day with his good friend Clarence King, a golf pro, who he called 'Honey Bear.' It was a Sunday morning and I was still in my pajamas when he headed out for the day. I was standing in the door with my poodle under my arm when Curtis walked out. He turned around and walked back to the door and rubbed my belly. He told me, 'I love you more than life and I will see you later.' He called me on the cell phone to have me call Martha (Clarence's wife) to plan a date for the night. He said he wanted a date with us girls."

Bunny had a feeling that she could not shake. She recalled her feelings that day as the worst thing she could even express. "My feet were nailed to the ground. I had a horrible feeling, I just did not know what it was, which made it even worse."

Curtis Turner and Clarence King never made it back home that day. After not hearing from the two men, their wives became very concerned. "Martha and I had an idea that they had crashed," Bunny said. "When I heard car tires come up to the house, I told Martha they were dead. I was so concerned that Curtis had burned when they crashed. Curtis always had a fear of burning. I could only think of that right then."

The FAA report would later rule that the accident was due to pilot error. The twin-engine aircraft still had one engine running when it crashed to the ground. Clarence King died of a massive coronary before they even hit the ground. Curtis Turner was killed instantly upon impact.

Bunny Turner was not only facing the death of her husband but the arrival of a baby that was due in just a few weeks without her husband at her side. She gave birth to Curtis Jr. on October 22, only 18 days after her husband lost his life.

Life changed dramatically for the young widow. The longtime dream of a new track fell apart as did many other aspects of her husband's business enterprises. She did not have many friends in racing so life was quite lonely. She relied on her brother, Danny, who became her "rock" and her other close friends and family.

Thirty-two years have passed since the death of Bunny's beloved husband. "I still think of him all the time and there are some things that Curtis Jr. will do that remind me of his dad," said Bunny. What she remembers the most about him was his love and appreciation for pure, raw nature and his personality. "There was a side to Curtis that most people did not get to see. He dripped with charisma! He was a very smart businessman and such a good person. The best advice he ever gave me was, 'Do not ever burn a bridge; you never know when you might have to walk back over it.'"

Today, Bunny resides in Christiansburg, Va., with her husband, Tommy Hall.

Curtis Jr. is married, lives close by with his wife, Missy, and their two children and once entertained thoughts of following in his dad's "racing footsteps." Today, though, he's the general manager of Sheelor Motor Mile, a large chain of auto dealerships based in Christiansburg.

Maura, who was born in December 1998, and Garret, who will celebrate his first birthday in September 2002, are Bunny's greatest pride and joy.

CURTIS MORTON TURNER

Curtis M. Turner, born April 12, 1924, in Floyd County, Va., was a larger-than-life personality — a person older fans of NASCAR racing talk about as if they knew him personally and the type of driver some modern-day race followers wish was racing today.

In a Winston Cup career that spanned 20 years, Turner competed in just 170 races and won 17, including the 1956 Southern 500 at Darlington, S.C. But he also dropped out of 90, mainly because of his style of driving — push the car as hard as possible and if it didn't last the entire race, so be it.

Turner was risk taker, buyer and seller of timberlands, alleged moonshine runner and much more. He was known as much for his all-night parties as for his feats on the track. NASCAR President Bill France Sr. enlisted his help on occasion, banned him from the sport for four years and ultimately called him the "greatest race car driver I have ever seen."

Turner ran what he called his first "real" race in 1946 at Mount Airy, N.C., finishing last in a field of 18 cars. But he caught on quickly and won his second race, which kicked off his reputation as one of the all-time great dirt-track drivers. At first, he was billed as Virginia's "Blond Blizzard," but he picked up the moniker "Pops" because of the way he popped the competition off the track.

What's today the NASCAR Winston Cup Series kicked off in 1949 with eight races and Turner ran six and won at Langhorne, Pa., in September. The next season he ran 16 races, won four and followed that up with three wins in 11 starts, in 1951. In all, he won about 360 races (NASCAR and others).

Turner also was a co-partner in the building of Charlotte Motor Speedway. When the project ran short of funds, he went to the Teamsters Union and agreed to try and organize the drivers in return for a loan. The project failed and France kicked him out of NASCAR. He was reinstated in late 1965, in time for him to win the first Winston Cup race at the new Rockingham, N.C., track.

Turner died Oct. 4, 1970 when the plane he was piloting crashed in rural Pennsylvania.

BUFFY WALTRIP

*B*orn in Monroe, La., in 1967, the youngest in a family of three children, Elizabeth "Buffy" Franks spent many of her formative years in Michigan and North Carolina. She and Michael Waltrip had crossed paths several times before they became an item. Theirs was a romance that blossomed in a hospital room, in 1988 — but not until they were friends first.

She first met her future husband at the Sandwich Construction Company, a restaurant on the north side of Charlotte, N.C. With everything from driver's suits to parts of Winston Cup Series cars on display, it was probably the first racing-themed eatery of its type in the country. The job was convenient because it was just a stone's throw from the University of North Carolina at Charlotte, where she was pursuing a degree in business.

"Michael would come in there from time to time. I did not have a racing background, so when the racing people would come in, they were no different to me than anyone else because I didn't know who they all were," Buffy recalled. "I was also going to school at the time working on my degree at UNCC, so I was pretty involved in college living. It was a good thing we didn't date at that time because it allowed me to enjoy my college years.

"Once I got out of school I went to work for a software company. I would run into Michael from time to time but nothing big. We were both unattached at the same time and kind of running in the singles scene at the same places."

Buffy then was hired by Sports Image, a company that produced and marketed licensed apparel such as driver and team T-shirts, caps and related items. The job also included work with a NASCAR-related General Motors program, which meant she had to attend races. There, she'd "hang out" with Michael, as they'd become "pretty good friends."

"It all changed for me with Michael at the Michigan race weekend in August 1992," she said. "I had to leave the track to take someone to the airport so I was not there when Michael wrecked pretty bad and had to be taken to the hospital in Jackson. I didn't get back to my hotel until about 9 p.m. Someone called to tell me that Michael had wrecked and that she thought I would want to know. I drove to the hospital to see him. When I got there, he was alone and resting. I remember thinking, here is this guy with this great career and he has no one. I stayed with him until around 2 a.m. It was that night that I realized that I felt different about him. We started dating pretty seriously after that."

(Left) The future Mrs. Waltrip: Elizabeth "Buffy" Franks was born in the "Pelican State" but grew into adulthood living in Michigan and North Carolina. (Opposite page) Daughter "Macy" is the apple of her mother's eye.

Macy came along in September 1997 and, according to Buffy, fit right in to the world of professional motorsports. Thanks to the conveniences available to contemporary racing families, caring for a child is much easier than it was 20 years ago.

On April, 3 1993 at Bristol (Tenn.) International Raceway, Buffy got a huge surprise in victory lane — and it wasn't the winner's trophy. Instead, it was a marriage proposal in front of thousands of people!

"It was a hard weekend for everybody," she recalled. Alan Kulwicki had died two days earlier so we all had a lot on our minds. *(Editor's Note: The defending Winston Cup Series champion perished in a plane crash while en route to the track.)* I think it made everybody realize what they had in their own lives. Michael won the Busch race that night (Saturday) and when he did, I ran to victory lane to meet him. When he was giving his interview, he pulled me up there and said, 'This is my girlfriend, Buffy.' I thought he just wanted to kind of make it official that he had a girlfriend. He then said, 'I want to marry her one-day.' Benny Parsons said,

'Hey Michael did you just ask her to marry you?' Michael looked at me and said, 'Will you marry me?' I said yes and then Michael said he had the ring in the truck. I laughed so hard later because I knew he meant it was in the hauler. It sounded so funny to hear Michael say, 'Yeah, the ring's in my truck.' Michael had 'happy hour' (final practice session) after that for the Winston Cup race, so I had to sit there at the hauler and wonder where my ring was until it was over. It was torture."

(Left) Caitlin Marie, who was born in 1990, and Buffy have developed a strong relationship since Buffy's marriage to Michael.

(Below) Because of her upbringing and the fact that her dad traveled, Buffy said she's adjusted well to a schedule that keeps her on the road with her husband much of the year. She and Michael, she said, are a team.

Michael and Buffy were married November 27, 1993 in Davidson, N.C. "We wanted to have a special wedding for our friends and family. It was just what we wanted," she said. "It was funny. Some of my friends asked me if I could handle traveling everywhere with Michael.

(Below) The Waltrips
returned to victory lane at
Daytona International
Speedway in February
2002 after Michael won
one of the Twin 125-Mile
Qualifying Races.

(Opposite page) Victory
lane there the year before
was bittersweet. Michael
had just won one of the
biggest events in the nation
but had lost his team
owner in the race.

I think my childhood got me ready for my current situation. My dad worked for a corporation. He was a successful businessman, so we moved a lot. I saw different things and went a lot of places so I like to move around like we do racing every weekend."

Michael was living in a 200-year-old farmhouse on 56 acres in Sherrills Ford, N.C., when he met Buffy. She found the idea of living in such a historic place "exciting" but knew she had a major project in front of her. After all, what works for a bachelor doesn't necessarily fit a woman's idea of proper décor.

"We renovated the house and added a pool. There is always something or some kind of project going on with our home. It is work in progress," she said.

Buffy and Michael were elated to find out they were going to have their first child together. Michael already had a daughter, Caitlin Marie, who was born in January 1990, and she was equally excited. Margaret "Macy" Carol was born Sept. 29, 1997. Thanks to modern conveniences, things didn't change that much for the Waltrips. Buffy, in fact, marveled at how much easier her life on the road is than it was for some of the racing wives of years ago.

"Macy goes with us a lot," Buffy said. "Everything has changed from motorhomes to jets and so on. It certainly makes it easy for all of us with children. This life on the road is so workable. I have no complaints. We have two of everything from toys to clothes, one at home and one on the motorhome. We are so blessed to have it like we do now. If we have done anything in this sport, we've made it as family friendly as possible. Having a child of my own made my life so complete. I feel that I have a very fulfilled life."

Michael and Buffy are very open about their religious beliefs. Buffy commends the Motor Racing Outreach ministry for her spiritual growth. "For the first time in my life when I leave church, I feel like I have learned something. They've helped to make me so hungry for the word of God," she said. "I believe anyone could go to a MRO service and come out a more mature Christian. They are that good at what they do. They are such a blessing for my family

and for the whole sport. I don't know how I'd stand it without them in our lives week in and week out."

Faith is what Buffy feels got her and Michael through one of the most difficult experiences in their lives. After countless years in NASCAR racing, Michael finally captured his first Winston Cup points-race win, the 2001 Daytona 500. His good friend and car owner, Dale Earnhardt, however, wasn't there to give him that congratulatory pat on the back. While Michael was heading toward the checkered flag, Dale lost his life in a last-lap accident.

"We were so close to Dale and Teresa. We vacationed with them several times a year. I was so full of pain," Buffy recalled. "Not only had Dale died but also Michael would not get to share his win with him. I'm so grateful for the time we had together as families and friends. Dale was amazing to Michael and me. When we would vacation with them, he would wait on you hand and foot. It was so funny to see him that way.

"Michael and I will never get over that day, but we know Dale is in a good place because he was a good man. I would be lying if I said last year did not get to me because it did. I felt like my life was on a screen watching it play out to a bad ending. But with many prayers we got through it."

Buffy stays involved in the day-to-day business of racing and Michael's career. They treat their marriage as a partnership and are, in essence, a team.

Buffy, however, would enjoy venturing into a business of her own but knows that's not possible at present. "I'd love to own my own restaurant but know I can't do that being gone like I am," she said. "So, I think I'm going to open up a high-end shoe store around the lake area where we live. I've been researching it and think it's something that I would enjoy and still be able to fly out on the weekends to be with Michael. The busier I am, the better."

Michael and Buffy are also keeping a close eye on Michael's big brother, Darrell. The three-time Winston Cup champion retired as a driver at the end of 2000 and is now a race analyst for FOX TV. Michael just might want to pursue television broadcasting, too, when his racing career ends.

"Michael has done some TV work and did real well with it," Buffy noted. "It's something in the back of our mind, as he gets a little older. I don't know what direction for sure we will go. But I can tell you that when Michael does retire, I want to be somewhere where it is warm. I want to be one of those people you see on the golf course wearing those plaid pants playing golf in the warm January sunshine. That would be the life!"

MICHAEL WALTRIP

While Michael Waltrip's inspiration to become a race car driver may be due in part to his being Darrell Waltrip's brother, that's about all the connection ever meant. By the time Michael was born on April 30, 1963 in Owensboro, Ky., his brother (who would go on to become a three-time NASCAR Winston Cup Series champion) was already 16 and tasting competition on local ovals.

The younger Waltrip began racing Go-Karts in the 1970s and after numerous victories switched to stock cars in 1981. He took the Mini-Modified Division championship at Kentucky Motor Speedway in 1982, began competing in the NASCAR Goody's Dash Series and won the championship in 1983 and was the series' Most Popular Driver in '83 and '84.

Waltrip made his Winston Cup Series debut in 1985 in May at Lowe's Motor Speedway with team owner Dick Bahre, starting 24th and finishing 28th. He ran four more races that year, went full time in '86 and finished second in rookie of the year points. Chuck Rider became the team's majority owner in 1988, renamed it Bahari Racing and Waltrip recorded his best finish to date, second at Pocono, Pa., in June.

Waltrip remained with Bahari through 1995 and then joined the venerable and prestigious Wood Brothers Racing organization in 1996. He recorded 11 top-10 finishes in 31 starts and won The Winston "all-star" event in May at Charlotte. In doing so, he became the first driver to win the race after transferring into it from the Winston Open. That year, he also went over the million-dollar mark in earnings for the first time.

After three seasons with the Woods, Waltrip left and drove for owner Jim Mattei in 1999 and half of 2000. He finished the 2000 season with Jim Smith's team and was tapped to drive for Dale Earnhardt's DEI, Inc. team in 2001. The year was bittersweet for Waltrip, as he won the Daytona 500 but lost his car owner, who died in a last-lap crash in that race.

Waltrip is also active in Busch Series racing. He has his own team and between 1988-2001 has won eight of 161 races.

AUTOGRAPHS